STOP RUSHING
Start Living

SIMPLE
WISDOM
PUBLISHING

© 2025 Liz Anderson. All rights reserved.

This material, including all content, is the exclusive property of Liz Anderson and is protected under copyright law. Unauthorised use, reproduction, modification, distribution, transmission, replication, or any form of dissemination of this Material, in whole or in part, without explicit prior written consent from the copyright owner, is strictly prohibited and may result in legal action.

Exceptions to this prohibition are limited to brief quotations for the purpose of reviews, scholarly analysis, or other similar non-commercial uses, as permitted under copyright law. Such usage must be accompanied by proper attribution to the copyright owner.

Requests for permission to use, reproduce, or distribute any part of this material should be directed to the copyright owner at the following address: PO Box 4124 Forest Lake QLD 4078 Australia. Email: slowdownwithliz@gmail.com

By accessing, viewing, or using this material, you acknowledge and agree to abide by these terms. Any infringement of these copyright terms may lead to legal proceedings, seeking remedies including but not limited to injunctive relief, damages, and recovery of legal costs.

Under no circumstances will any blame or legal responsibility be held against the publisher, or author, for any damages, reparation, or monetary loss due to the information contained within this book including, but not limited to – errors, omissions, or inaccuracies. Either directly or indirectly.

A catalogue record for this book is available from the National Library of Australia.

Cover design by Turtle Publishing
Interior layout by Turtle Publishing
Photography by Liz Anderson

Disclaimer

This book contains general information intended for educational purposes only and draws on widely available concepts in psychology and self-help. Although all care has been taken in compiling the contents, this book does not take into account individual circumstances and is not in any way a substitute for medical or professional mental health advice. Always consult a qualified practitioner. Neither the author, the publisher, nor their distributors can be held responsible for any loss, claim or action that may arise from reliance on the information contained in this book. Readers should seek professional advice where appropriate.

Transparency Note

This book was written with care and intention by me, drawing on my personal and professional experience. I used AI tools as part of the creative process, for brainstorming, refining wording, and editing, much like an author might use an editor, research assistant, or thesaurus. Every idea, story, and teaching here reflects my own voice, expertise, and perspective.

First published by Simple Wisdom Publishing 2025

ISBN: 978-1-7641288-3-0 (ebook)
ISBN: 978-1-7641288-1-0 (paperback)
ISBN: 978-1-7641288-2-7 (audio book)

*To everyone who's ever felt
like life is moving too fast,
may you find the courage to
slow down and truly live.*

Table of Contents

ACKNOWLEDGEMENTS — vii
INTRODUCTION — ix
GETTING THE MOST FROM THIS BOOK — xiii

Slow Living: What It Is And Isn't — 1

The History Of Slow Living — 3
Myths And Misconceptions — 4
The Guiding Principles Of Slow Living — 8

Living On Purpose: The Power Of Intention — 15

Intention vs Goals - What's The difference? — 17
How To Set Meaningful Intentions — 18
Different Ways To Set Intentions — 21
Practical Exercise: Setting Your Intentions For The Day — 25

Right Here, Right Now: The Power Of Presence — 31

What It Really Means To Be Present — 33
What Mindfulness Can Do For You — 34
Mindfulness vs. Meditation: What's The Difference? — 35
How Do I Become Mindful? — 35
Ten Mindfulness Techniques — 40
Mindful Moments All Day Long — 46

Everyday Grace: Finding Joy & Gratitude In The Ordinary — 51

What Is Gratitude? — 53
Three Key Aspects of Gratitude — 54
What If I Can't Find Anything To Be Grateful For? — 56
Can Noticing The Little Things Really Make A Difference? — 57
Simple Ways To Add Gratitude Into Your Day — 59
Practical Exercises: Experiencing Gratitude in Action — 62

Self-Care: The Art of Looking After You — 65

Self-Care Isn't Selfish. Here's Why — 66
Talking About Self-Care With Sceptics — 68
40 Self-Care Practices To Nourish Your Mind, Body And Soul — 71
Practical Exercise: Making Your Own Self-Care Menu — 74

Simplify, Unclutter & Thrive — 79

Why Enough Never Feels Like Enough — 81
Why Simplify My Life? — 82
I'm Convinced! So Where Do I Start? — 83
Decluttering Your Mind — 91
Your Sanctuary: A Tool For Mental Clarity — 92
Practical Exercise: Create Your Mini-Sanctuary — 96

Disconnect to Reconnect: The Path Back to You — 101

Why It's Important To Unplug	103
Making Space for Deeper Thinking and Creativity	104
How Do I Unplug And Reconnect?	106
Practical Exercise: Getting Comfortable With Silence	113

The Power Of Boundaries: Creating Space For What Matters — 117

The Struggles Of A People-Pleaser	120
General Tips For Boundary Setting	124
Practical Ideas for Setting Boundaries	128
Practical Exercise: Creating Boundaries That Stick	141

Learning to Let Go — 145

Why Is Letting Go So Hard?	147
Why Is It Important?	148
OK, So How Do I Let Go?	149
Acceptance	151
Where Does Forgiveness Fit In?	151
Letting Go Of The Things You Can't Change	153
Techniques For Letting Go	157
How Often Do I Have To Let It Go?	166
Practical Exercise: Let's Write A Letter	167

The Power of Self-Reflection — 171

What Is Self-Reflection?	173
Building A Better Relationship With You	174

Being Emotionally Responsible — 175
Self-Reflection: How To Do It — 176
Practical Exercise: My Check-In Questions — 177

How to Make Lasting Change — 181

But Why Is Change So Hard? — 183
The Stages of Change: Why Change Happens In Phases — 184
The Grey Zone — 186
The Pros And Cons Of Making Change — 188
Tips For Building Habits That Last — 190
Not Everyone Will Cheer You On, And That's Okay — 193
Practical Exercise: Weighing The Pros And Cons of Change — 196

When To Seek Professional Help — 199

How Can Therapy Help Me? — 201
Finding The Right Therapist — 203
How Often Should I Go? — 207

Let's Get Started: Your Slow Living Roadmap — 211

From Ideas To Action — 214
Your Slow Living Roadmap — 215
It's Time For Some Tough Love — 224

Final Thoughts — 227

NOTE TO THE READER — 229
REFERENCES — 231

ACKNOWLEDGEMENTS

First and foremost, I want to thank my wonderful husband who has always supported me in everything I do. No matter what wild idea I dream up, he meets it with encouragement, patience, and unwavering belief in me. You are my rock, my steady partner in crime, and I couldn't imagine this journey without you by my side.

To my two amazing boys, you make your dad and I the luckiest parents alive. You are thoughtful, kind, and awesome to be around. Thank you for your patience on all those nights when I was writing and we had leftovers (again!) without complaint. Your love and easy-going spirits mean the world to me.

To my parents, thank you for your constant love, encouragement, and unwavering support throughout my life. You nurtured my curiosity about life's mysteries and planted the seeds of my passion for helping others discover their inner strength.

To my brother, you are my best friend. Your unfiltered advice, steady support, and shared passion for all things spiritual and esoteric have been invaluable. I am so grateful for our deep connection and the way you've walked this path with me.

To my dear friend and fellow psychologist, Fabienne, your friendship, honest feedback, and professional wisdom have guided me through this book and life itself. I am deeply thankful for you and all your support over the years.

To Tania, my spiritual advisor, thank you for always being direct, encouraging, and positive. You've helped me navigate self-doubt, learn to believe in myself and trust my intuition and inner guidance.

And to all the other wonderful people who have touched my life, whether in big ways or small, thank you. I've been privileged to learn from your own journeys of self-discovery, and this book is also written in honour of you.

And finally, to you, the reader. Thank you for walking this path with me. My hope is that these pages offer inspiration, comfort, practical guidance and serve as a gentle companion on your own path to a slower, richer, and more meaningful life.

From the bottom of my heart, thank you all.

INTRODUCTION

"Time is a precious gift. Use it wisely."

— Liz Anderson

My first encounter with the concept of slow living happened one morning a few years ago. Coffee in hand, half-listening to the news while mindlessly scrolling on my phone. Most of the segment washed over me until one word made me stop: burnout. The presenter described slow living as an antidote to the constant rush of modern life. A way to step out of the cycle of stress and exhaustion and create a more intentional life that was balanced and more in line with what makes your heart sing. In that moment, it was as if someone had finally put into words how I'd been feeling for years but was too busy to acknowledge.

I'd been questioning the pace of my life for a while, knowing that deep down things needed to change but always putting it on the back burner, another thing to look at when I had the time. But that morning, I had a revelation. I realised how often I was putting things on hold. I'd fallen into the familiar trap of 'I'll be happy when...' When I lose weight, when I get more organised, when I finally have more time. But none of that was happening. I was constantly waiting for life to settle down but that time never came. I was stuck in a cycle of busyness, watching my life fly by from the sidelines.

My children, who only yesterday were newborns, were suddenly teenagers, my oldest on the brink of graduating from high school, venturing out into the wide world and my youngest already halfway through his high school journey. I kept wondering, where did all that time go? A week would pass in the blink of an eye, yet when I tried to recall what happened just seven days ago, it felt like a lifetime had passed.

You know, it's funny, I've noticed that whenever I'm going through something, I start to see it mirrored all around me. Articles, conversations, podcasts, and even social media posts on that topic pop up everywhere. Maybe it's just the algorithm, but I like to think it's the universe giving me a gentle nudge, saying, "Pay attention".

So, I listened and followed the nudge. I started researching slow living and quickly found myself deep in a world of websites, podcasts, and YouTube channels. There are whole communities of people exploring this beautiful, countercultural idea. The more I read and listened, the more I realised these were the very strategies I'd been teaching my clients for decades as a psychologist. I'd long encouraged others to pause, to reflect, to simplify, to live more intentionally, but somewhere along the way, I'd stopped following my own advice.

It's so much easier to help other people change their lives than it is to take an honest look at your own behaviours. I knew I couldn't keep doing the same things and expect different results, so little by little, I began to follow the principles of slow living and things started to change. I felt calmer, more connected, less overwhelmed and more in control. Life felt sacred again, full of richness, presence, and meaning.

This transformation, still ongoing, inspired me to write this book, because I know I'm not alone. I've seen the same burnout, the same longing for a slower, more meaningful, and more manageable life reflected in my clients, my friends, and in the world around me. Now more than ever, in an uncertain world, this way of living is essential. It brings us back to basics and keeps us connected to what's important.

This book is for anyone who feels life is moving too fast and who longs to slow down, breathe, and make room for the things that bring joy and meaning.

Here's what you can expect to learn:
- A clear sense of what slow living looks like for you.
- Practical ways to simplify your life, set boundaries, and reclaim your time and energy.
- Tools for saying no and dealing with resistance from others.
- How to find joy in the small things and develop real gratitude.
- Guidance for learning to let go of expectations, clutter, past hurts, and habits that no longer serve you.

- Mindfulness strategies you can actually use (without needing to meditate for an hour a day).
- How to develop habits that last.
- How to use the power of intention to change your life.

GETTING THE MOST FROM THIS BOOK

Just as slow living invites us to move through life with intention and care, I encourage you to approach this book in the same way, unhurried, mindful and open-hearted.

My suggestion is to begin by reading through the entire book at your own pace to develop a feel for its ideas and themes. Then, go back and revisit each chapter one week at a time. This slower approach allows you to absorb the insights deeply, reflect on the content, and give yourself the space to experiment with the exercises and practices in real life.

At the end of each chapter, you'll find a Challenge and an Affirmation for the Week. These are designed for you to integrate what you've learned into your weekly routine and gently reinforce the mindset shifts that support your slow living journey.

By investing in yourself now, you're creating a foundation for a more manageable and fulfilling future. You will have the inner tools to handle whatever comes your way with calmness and confidence. Instead of being pulled along by external events and people, you will be centred, capable, and in charge of your own choices and pathway.

This journey is deeply personal and completely individual. You don't have to make any big life-changing decisions. It starts with small, simple shifts, one step at a time.

But beware! This book isn't a quick fix. It asks for your participation, your reflection, and your willingness to make small but meaningful changes.

So, if you're ready to stop rushing and start living, this book is for you! Take a deep breath, slow down, and let's begin, one mindful step at a time.

CHAPTER 1

Slow Living: What It Is And Isn't

> *"The faster we go, the less we see."*
> — Unknown

A few years ago, I found myself standing in my kitchen, reheating yet another round of leftovers while scrolling through work emails on my phone. My teenage sons sat at the bench beside me, silently eating with their earbuds in, barely registering my presence. I looked up for a moment and, for the first time, really looked at everything in the space around me. I saw the fridge crowded with school notes and appointment reminders, the bench strewn with unopened mail, the hum of busy lives lived side by side but not quite together.

Our schedule was overflowing. Our days were full. And yet... I felt like something was missing. We were always doing, always moving, always chasing the next thing. Ticking boxes, crossing off to-do lists. We were living life but not stopping to enjoy and savour it.

I kept telling myself I shouldn't complain. Every working mum I knew was carrying the same load, and, as a psychologist, wasn't I meant to have everything figured out? Shouldn't I have all the solutions and strategies to life mastered? But I kept going around in circles thinking, surely there's more to life than this? I don't want to feel like I'm constantly chasing my tail, but where do I start and what do I do? Anyway, I don't have time to think about this right now, I have to do the dishes, make dinner, write that report, pay that bill. The list was never ending!

My sense that something had to change grew stronger by the day, taking up more and more space in my thoughts. Those deep self-probing questions were persistent always sitting in the back of my mind as I went through my day. They were there as I lingered over morning coffees; they surfaced while I scrolled aimlessly on my phone; and they whispered in my ear in the quiet moments before sleep. I didn't have any answers yet, just a steady inner knowing that something needed to shift.

That fateful morning when I discovered slow living was my turning point, my wake-up call. It wasn't a grand "Aha" moment, but something clicked into place and I knew it was the beginning of what I'd been seeking. A new way of living.

And in a lovely twist of synchronicity, my first awareness of needing change arose in my kitchen, the very place where the slow living movement itself began.

Because before it was a lifestyle, a mindset, or a philosophy, slow living started with something simple and essential: food.

The History Of Slow Living

The slow living movement grew out of the slow food movement which began in Italy in the 1980s. Italians have always taken food seriously, very seriously. Home-cooked food doesn't just feed the body, it nourishes the mind and the soul. It's a source of connection, cultural identity, community and celebration. Gathering around the table with loved ones is a cherished ritual, a time to share stories, pass down traditions, and nurture a deep sense of belonging.

But when fast food chains began appearing across Italy, many feared that something bigger than eating habits was changing. Instead of lingering in the kitchen, learning from one another and connecting through shared meals, people, especially younger generations, were choosing convenience. In doing so, they were losing the richness of time spent together as a family and the wisdom that their older generations had to offer. Fast food, they feared, wasn't just speeding up mealtimes; it was eroding family life, personal connection, and the heart of cultural identity.

This dilemma inspired Carlo Petrini to develop the concept of slow food which, amongst other things, championed traditional food practices, respect for local growers, and a return to high-quality, seasonal ingredients. But more than that, it was a statement that some things are too important to rush. The idea of slow was born: slow cooking, slow enjoyment and slow time together. Over time, this idea of slow has grown to influence all other areas of life too.

Today, the slow living movement encourages us to shift from a life of chronic busyness to one rooted in mindfulness, intention, and depth. It invites us to become more aware of our thoughts, our emotions, our habits, and how our choices affect our well-being. When we begin to slow down, we create space for clarity, connection, and a renewed appreciation for life's simplest pleasures.

Before we explore the guiding principles of slow living, let's clear up the common myths and misconceptions that arise when people first hear about this way of living.

Myths And Misconceptions

It's a Curated Look

One of the main misconceptions about slow living is that many people think it's about a curated aesthetic, perfectly arranged breakfasts, minimalist homes, off-grid living, and Instagram-worthy moments of serenity. We've all seen the reels, someone effortlessly sipping tea in a sunlit kitchen, tending to a lush garden or journaling by candlelight. Sure, these scenes look peaceful and inviting, and yes, they can be part of slow living, but what about real life?

What happens when your kids are screaming at each other? Or you've just finished a gruelling twelve-hour shift? Or you're stuck in your third meeting of the day with a group of annoying people? Or worse yet, stuck in peak hour traffic moving at a snail's pace, and you're desperate to pee? The truth is, slow living is a mindset, a shift in our thinking to match our values, doing what's truly important to us and letting go of unnecessary stress and the things we can't control.

Living Slowly Involves Taking Your Time

The goal of slow living is not to put things off or to go very slowly. Apart from this being very frustrating and counter-productive, it's more about concentrating your energies on the things that are important to you in order to improve and enrich your life. The goal is to work smarter, not harder, so that you can spend more time with the people you love and doing the things you're passionate about.

Only The Privileged Can Live Slowly

Slow living isn't about where you live or how much you earn. It's about your mindset. In fact, research consistently shows that the greatest contributors to happiness aren't wealth or status, but things like strong relationships, a sense of purpose, and the ability to savour the present moment. These are the very foundations of a slower, more intentional life, and the best part is they're free and available to anyone.

Slow Living Means Having No Hustle or Moving To The Countryside

Choosing to live a more intentional and slower life doesn't mean giving up on success. Many people think it means moving to the countryside to make jams, grow your own veggies, and raise some chickens. Yes, this might be heaven to some people but purgatory for others. Many high-achieving professionals actively embrace slow living as a way to prevent burnout, boost creativity, and increase productivity. This mindset and way of life can be practised anywhere: in a busy city, a small-town suburb, or a high-rise apartment. It's not about where you live, but how you live.

Slow Living Means Avoiding Technology

Slow living isn't about rejecting technology or pretending it has no place in our lives. Instead, it's about recognising that technology is a tool that can enrich and support us when used with care, rather than something that consumes, controls and numbs us from being conscious in the present moment. It invites us to use our devices with intention, choosing moments that add value, connection, or ease, instead of letting screens become a way to fill empty spaces or distract us.

You Can't Be Productive While Living Slowly

Slow living doesn't mean doing less. Rather it encourages us to pause, reflect and simplify where we can. Can we get help? Can we delegate? Do we need to be doing it at all? I'm sorry to say, you'll still need to iron clothes, scrub the toilet, and probably go to work. But can you do things differently to give yourself more time to recharge your batteries and increase the joy in life? There are numerous studies showing that productivity is actually increased when people feel happy and have a sense of meaning and purpose. So by reducing stress, avoiding burnout, and working with your natural energy levels, you can actually become more productive, focused, and creative.

Slow Living is Only About Self-care and Relaxation

Many people think slow living is just about self-care, having bubble baths, getting massages and sipping on tea while looking wistfully off into the sunset. And yes, self-care does indeed play an important role in slow living, but it's about so much more than indulging ourselves. It's a holistic approach to life, finding balance in all things.

You Have to Follow a Strict Set of Rules

Definitely not. There's no right way to practise the concepts of slow living. Take the tips and suggestions from this book that resonate with you and tweak them. Adapt them to fit your life. Some practices will work well and others not so much and that's okay; we're all different. Practising slow living should enhance your life, not leave you feeling flustered, stressed or not good enough.

The Guiding Principles Of Slow Living

Now that we've cleared up what slow living isn't, let's take a closer look at what it is. These guiding principles aren't strict rules you must follow; think of them as gentle signposts to help you shape a more sustainable, fulfilling, and joy-filled life.

Live Intentionally

Intention drives the universe. That's a bold statement, but I truly believe it to be true. It shapes our choices, influences our actions, and impacts our experiences. Intentional living enables us to move through life with purpose and awareness, taking ownership of our time, energy, and emotions. It ensures that our actions align with our values and what's important to us. Being intentional encourages us to pause and ask ourselves, "Why am I doing this? Why is this important to me? What am I hoping will happen?"

Be Present

In a world that constantly demands our attention, mindfulness brings us back to the here and now. When we're fully present, we begin to notice the little things that so often pass us by, the warmth of the sun on our skin, the way the leaves of a tree move in the wind, the comforting aroma of a home-cooked meal. These are the simple, beautiful moments that make life rich and meaningful. Mindfulness acts like a time machine, slowing things down and stretching out the space between moments giving us room to stop, breathe, and feel. It reconnects us with ourselves and the world around us.

Gratitude

Gratitude is the practice of acknowledging and appreciating what we have. The people, moments, and comforts that make life meaningful. By training our mind to notice what supports and enriches us, especially in busy or challenging times, we build our emotional resilience. This is your ability to bounce back from stress, setbacks, or challenges. Gratitude shifts our focus from what's missing or overwhelming to what is steady and sustaining. Creating a sense of contentment that eases the pressures of daily life and makes space for more joy and connection.

Self-care

When we intentionally rest, recharge, and tend to our own well-being, we're better equipped to show up, calm, clear, and present, for the people and responsibilities in our lives. Self-care isn't a luxury. It's an essential practice that restores our energy, nurtures our creativity and keeps us strong and steady through life's ups and downs.

Prioritise Quality Over Quantity

When we focus on quality over quantity, we create space for richer experiences, more clarity, and a deeper sense of fulfilment. We shift our focus from doing more and having more to our experiences and relationships. We choose better, whether it's how we spend our time, who we spend it with, or the possessions we bring into our homes.

Embrace Simplicity

Life is rarely straightforward. Just when things are serene and settled and we breathe a little easier the universe tosses us a curveball. Chaos and calm dance together in an ongoing rhythm. Change is the only constant which is why bringing simplicity into our daily routines and physical environment is essential. When our lives are not filled up with extraneous demands and possessions we can think clearly and see around us with greater ease. While real peace begins within, it's far easier to find and hold onto when our outer world supports it, rather than competes for our attention.

Disconnect to Reconnect

Slow living encourages us to step back from the noise of modern life, seek silence and spend more time in nature, where our senses can relax and our thoughts can wander. Nature doesn't have to mean a remote forest; it can be your garden, a local park, or even a sunny spot on your balcony. Silence makes room for inspiration to strike, for clarity to return, and gives us the space to reconnect to ourselves, others and the world around us.

Setting Boundaries

You can't truly slow down or create space for what matters if life is constantly dragging you from one thing to the next, leaving you feeling stretched thin and out of control. Learning to say no to what doesn't serve you, inspire you, or align with what you care about is not selfish; it's powerful. When you honour your limits, you're not just protecting your time and energy, you're reminding yourself (and those around you) that your life and your well-being are worth protecting.

Make Space To Reflect

Taking time to reflect helps us tune into our inner world. When we become aware of our thoughts, we can actually feel them, sit with them, and begin to understand what they're trying to tell us. It's in these quiet, honest moments that we gain clarity about our needs, desires, and the areas of our life calling out for attention.

Learning To Let Go

I also wanted to include learning to let go as part of the slow living journey. In life, there are two kinds of things: those we can control and those we can't. We have control over our own actions, choices, and how we respond to situations, but we can't control how others think, behave, or react. Nor can we control many of the external forces in the world. The news cycle, global events, economic shifts, or the unpredictable nature of life itself. Letting go is about learning to discern what's within our power and what isn't and finding peace in that realisation. When we let go of the illusion of control, we can begin to focus our energy on our mindset, our values and our choices.

Heartbeat Of The Chapter

At its heart, slow living is about creating a life that feels meaningful, balanced, and aligned with your values. It's about being intentional with your time and energy, focusing on what brings joy and value and letting go of what drains or distracts you. It's available to anyone, anywhere, at any stage of life. You don't need to buy acreage, quit your job, or splash out on a complete life overhaul. Transformative change begins with small, mindful choices that gather momentum over time.

I was 50 when I seriously committed to the principles of slow living, and the ripple effects have been remarkable. I've seen clients in their seventies and eighties start this journey too, and the spark in their eyes says it all. It's never too late to make changes.

So let's step onto this path together, one unhurried moment at a time, and discover just how expansive life becomes when we give ourselves permission to slow down.

Challenge This Week

Take some time to absorb everything we've covered so far.

Do a few internet searches and explore additional resources online on slow living. Watch some insightful videos, and allow yourself to stay curious and open-minded as you deepen your understanding of this new and exciting way of living and imagine how it might look for you.

Affirmation This Week

"I am learning to welcome change with an open heart and a curious mind. Trusting that every small step is guiding me toward growth and richer experiences."

CHAPTER 2

Living On Purpose: The Power Of Intention

"Purpose is the reason you journey. Intention is the map that guides you."

— Unknown

Before my slow living journey, I was often reluctant to exercise. Some days it felt like a chore, and I'd drag my feet, searching for any excuse to skip it. But the grown-up inside me knew I needed to exercise to be healthy, so I'd sigh, slip on my shoes, and brace myself for the walk ahead, already thinking about how quickly I could get it over with so I could move on to everything else on my to-do list.

As I stepped outside, I found myself rushing, checking the time, focused on finishing rather than experiencing it. My mind wandered to everything else I should be doing, and by the time I arrived back, I hadn't enjoyed a single moment of my walk. I just felt glad it was over.

But one morning, I decided to try something different. Instead of focusing on pace, distance, or time, I set the intention to simply enjoy my walk, to notice my surroundings, breathe deeply, and think of it as "me" time. That small shift in thinking completely changed my experience and highlighted to me how important setting your intention can be.

A walk is one of the simplest ways to see the power of intention in action. Your intention will be different depending on what matters to you in that moment. Some days, it might be about fitness, and you focus on a heart-pumping challenge. Other days, it might be about slowing down, noticing the world around you, or reconnecting with yourself. The same walk can lead to very different experiences depending on your intention at the time.

This is the transformative power of intention. By setting a clear intention before an activity, you become aware of why you're doing it, the purpose it serves, and the outcome you hope to achieve. You step out of autopilot and bring focus, clarity, and a greater sense of control to your actions and start to live more fully in the moment. Intention helps you reflect on whether your actions align with who you want to be and deepens your connection with yourself by helping you understand what motivates and is meaningful to you.

Whether it's how you begin your morning, navigate a challenging conversation, or approach your to-do list, intention guides your choices and shapes your experiences.

Intention vs Goals - What's The difference?

So how is an intention different from a goal? Aren't they basically the same thing? Not quite. While they're connected and can support each other, intentions and goals serve very different purposes. Let's look at some of them below:

Being vs. Doing

An intention is a way of being. It's a guide for how you want to live, rooted in your mindset and the values you care about. For example, you might say, "I intend to be patient in my interactions today." This isn't just about one day; it's about cultivating patience as a part of who you are.

Goals, on the other hand, are about doing and achieving. They focus on measurable outcomes like, "I'll write a chapter in my book today." Goals are completed and then replaced with new ones.

Intentions, however, stay with you; they quietly guide your choices and keep you aligned with your deeper values over time.

Flexible vs. Specific

Intentions are flexible. They can shift depending on what's most important to you in the moment. They're about living in alignment with your values, rather than hitting a particular mark. Whereas goals tend to be more specific, often measurable, and usually follow the SMART framework: Specific, Measurable, Achievable, Relevant, and Time-bound. Think about it this way: your intention is the compass, and your goals are the steps you take along the path.

Process vs. Outcome

Intentions focus on the journey. They remind you how you want to live, how you want to show up, and how you want to feel. Goals often focus on the destination. By anchoring your goals in intention, you bring a sense of purpose and meaning to each step, rather than chasing outcomes that might not be that important to you.

How Goals and Intentions Work Together

When your goals are guided by intention, they feel more meaningful, motivating, and connected to who you are. Setting intentions encourages you to pause and reflect, "Does this align with the life I want to live? Are my actions in line with what matters most to me?"

How To Set Meaningful Intentions

So now that we understand what intentions are and why they matter, how do we actually make meaningful ones? Do you have to set an intention before everything you do? Definitely not! That would be exhausting and unrealistic.

The real power of intention comes when you're doing something new, building a habit, or wanting to bring more meaning to an activity. And the good news is, once you've set an intention for something, you don't need to repeat it every time, just briefly reconnect with it, and it's there, ready to guide you. Unless the meaning of the activity changes for you, your original intention still holds.

Below are some simple tips to help you get the most out of setting your intentions.

Be Clear

Rather than being vague, state exactly what you want, for example, "I want to be more mindful in my day today."

Make sure your intentions are focused on what you can actually control. You can't set intentions for other people. You can only guide your own thoughts, choices, and actions, so keep your intention personal, specific, and rooted in your values and behaviour.

Keep It Simple

You don't need to create a long list of intentions to live by every single day, that's a fast track to overwhelm. Instead, choose your intentions based on what your day holds. If you're spending the day at home, your intention might be, "I want to move through today with more mindfulness." If you're at work all day tomorrow, you might set an intention like, "I will listen with patience and an open mind at work." Let your intentions support your day, not add pressure to it.

Remind Yourself Of Your Intentions

I've literally said to myself, "My intention today is..." only to realise five minutes later that I've completely forgotten it. Life moves fast, and even when things are going smoothly, it's easy to let your intentions slip. When it's busy or overwhelming, that quiet commitment to yourself can vanish entirely.

That's why little reminders are so powerful. A note on the bathroom mirror that says, "Be kind," or a sticky note on the fridge with "Be mindful today" can bring you back to the bigger picture. These little anchors are not about micromanaging your day. Their purpose is to guide your choices and actions so you stay connected to the kind of life you want to live.

Follow Your Intention With Actions That Support It

Setting your intention is the first step but then you need to bring it to life through small, doable actions. Each time you act in alignment with your intention, you strengthen self-trust, build self-worth, and deepen your connection to your values. It's not about being perfect; it's about showing up with consistency and care, proving to yourself that you're committed to living with intention and purpose.

For example, if your intention is to bring more mindfulness into your day, you might start the morning with a few deep breaths or pause to feel the breeze on your skin while hanging out the washing, small doable actions done with greater awareness.

It's Not Always About You

Living with intention doesn't mean only following your own desires or saying no to anything you don't feel like doing. It's not about becoming self-centred. It's about making conscious choices that honour both your own needs and the needs of the people who matter to you.

Sometimes, living with intention means saying yes to things that aren't your personal favourite, not from guilt or obligation, but because they align with your values. You might not enjoy football, but you go to a game with your partner because you value quality time together. You might be tired, but you bake cupcakes with your child because you value presence and shared memories. And I don't know about you but getting my kids to do something when it suits my schedule is nearly impossible! So I count it as a win whenever they want to spend time with me, even if the timing isn't ideal.

When you show up for someone with presence and a full heart, those moments become meaningful rather than draining. That's the beauty of intentional living, it creates a balance between caring for yourself and nurturing your relationships. It's not just about what you do, but why you do it.

Different Ways To Set Intentions

There are so many ways to set intentions, and the key is finding one that feels natural and meaningful for you. In the next section, I'll share a few quick, simple techniques I've used both personally and with my clients. Some you can do in your head in a few moments; others invite you to slow down, reflect, and write things out.

While you don't have to write every intention down, in the beginning it can be especially helpful to do so. Putting pen to paper lets you explore what feels right, experiment with different approaches, and start shaping a method that's uniquely yours. With regular practice, intention-setting will start to feel natural, effortless, and part of the rhythm of your day.

The One-Sentence Intention Method

Before starting something new or building a new habit, take a moment to get clear on why you're doing it. State your intention in a single, clear sentence that connects the action you want to take with the deeper reason behind it.

For example:

- "My intention is to practice mindfulness so that I can feel calmer and more present."
- "My intention is to cook nourishing meals so that I can take care of my body and feel energised."
- "My intention is to move my body more so that I can move more freely."

These types of statements act like an anchor; they ground you in purpose, help you live in alignment with what's important to you and give you the clarity to follow through.

The Four-Question Intention Method

This method is a little more in-depth than the first one. Setting intentions becomes much easier when you have a simple way to clarify them. The questions below are designed to help you pause, reflect, and connect your intention to what's important to you in the moment. You can run through them in your head or jot down your answers. Either way, they'll help you move from a vague idea to a clear, purposeful action you can carry with you through your day.

1. What's my intention for today?
2. Why does this matter to me right now?
3. Which of my personal values does this support?
4. What's one simple action I can take to live this intention today?

For example:
1. **What's my intention for today?** To start a daily gratitude practice.
2. **Why does this matter to me right now?** Because I want to focus on what's already in my life instead of what's missing, and nurture a more positive mindset.
3. **Which of my personal values does this support?** Mindfulness, appreciation and emotional well-being.
4. **What's one simple action I can take to live this intention today?** I'll write down three things I'm grateful for.

When you take a moment to answer these questions, you're not just setting an intention; you're giving yourself a clear path to live it with purpose in a way that's meaningful to you.

Visualisation Method

Visualisation speaks directly to your subconscious, enabling you to believe deeply in your intentions and for them to guide your actions. It gives you a chance to see what living your intention could look like and that bringing it into reality can be simpler than you think; all it takes is attention and awareness.

You begin by bringing your intention to mind. Close your eyes and picture yourself living it. See it, feel it, and let yourself step into that moment as if it's happening right now.

For example, if your intention is to bring more gratitude into your day, imagine you're sitting at the kitchen table in the soft morning light, a warm cup of tea in your hands. The house is quiet. Your journal is open, ready for you to write. You feel a sense of peace as you think of the little things you're grateful for: a restful night's sleep, the song of birds outside, a meaningful conversation yesterday. You write them down, feeling each one settle warmly in your heart.

Notice how you feel in this moment. Peaceful, content, and grounded. Grounded is that sense of being anchored within yourself, calm, steady, and present, even when life pulls at you from all directions. Even if challenges come later, you carry this feeling with you, ready to meet the day with a clear and positive mind.

Practical Exercise: Setting Your Intentions For The Day

Each morning brings a fresh opportunity to decide how you want to move through your day, not by controlling every outcome, but by setting the tone for the life you want to experience. This exercise will help you begin creating a simple routine for setting your daily intentions and discovering what feels best for you. So let's dive in!

Step 1

As you go about your morning, whether you're brushing your teeth, making your coffee, or sitting quietly, take a moment to reflect on the day ahead. **Ask yourself:**

- What's happening in my day today?
- Are there any challenges or stressors I'm anticipating?
- What moments might bring joy, connection or meaning?

Maybe you have a packed schedule with back-to-back meetings. Maybe you're catching up with a friend you haven't seen in ages. Or maybe you're spending a quiet day at home, juggling family responsibilities.

Step 2

Now take a moment to ask yourself:

- How do I want to feel as I move through the day?
- What quality or mindset would I like to embody today?

Step 3

Now let's turn that reflection into a short, powerful intention statement, something that grounds you and gives you a sense of purpose for the day ahead.

Here are some examples to get you started:
- If you have a demanding workday ahead: "I intend to meet today's challenges with calm focus and steady energy."
- If you're feeling anxious or scattered: "I intend to move slowly and gently, giving myself permission to breathe."
- If you're dealing with family or emotional stress: "I intend to respond with patience and speak from a place of love."

Take a moment now to set your own intention for the day. Keep it short, clear, and personal. You can write it in your journal, note it on your phone, say it out loud, or hold it quietly in your heart. Nothing fancy, just a short statement to help guide your energy through the day.

Step 4

Now let's think about what actions you can take to make this intention come to life?

Here are some ideas to get you started:

Intention: "I intend to meet today's challenges with calm focus and steady energy."

Supporting action ideas:
- Start the morning with 5 minutes of quiet breathing or stretching.
- Take short breaks between meetings to reset my focus.
- Remind myself of my intention before starting a new task or conversation.

Intention: "I intend to move slowly and gently, giving myself permission to breathe."

Supporting action ideas:
- Say no to unnecessary commitments today.
- Walk instead of rushing, even for small things like getting a coffee or moving between rooms.
- Use a calming reminder (a post-it note, phone wallpaper, or an alarm) to check in with my breath.

Intention: "I intend to respond with patience and speak from a place of love."

Supporting action ideas:
- Pause and take one full breath before responding during stressful moments.
- Use a mantra like "just breathe" when I feel triggered.
- Reflect on one positive quality in the person I'm feeling tension with.

Take a moment now to write out some supporting actions you can take to support your intention.

The more you practice a technique like this, the more natural and effortless setting your intentions becomes. It will simply be part of your morning rhythm. In only a few minutes, you can set your mindset for the day ahead. It doesn't mean the day will be perfect, but it does mean you'll begin from a place of calmness and clarity, ready to meet whatever comes your way with steadiness instead of stress.

Heartbeat Of The Chapter

I hope this chapter has given you a deeper understanding of what intention is, why it matters, and how it differs from setting a goal. Intention shapes your experience. You can do the very same activity with two different intentions and walk away with completely different feelings, insights, or outcomes.

Your intentions act as a gentle compass, quietly guiding your actions, your focus, and the way you show up in everyday life. They help you stay aligned with your values and what's important to you and the beautiful thing is, living with intention doesn't require a complete life overhaul. It simply begins with a pause. A quiet moment to reflect and ask yourself, "What do I want this to mean?".

Challenge This Week

Choose one or two of the intention-setting ideas from this chapter and give them a try. If you're feeling keen, try one every morning! And at the end of the week, take a few moments to reflect on your experience.

- Did setting your intentions give you a clearer sense of purpose or direction?
- When you set an intention before an activity, did it shift how you experienced it or affect the outcome in any way?
- Can you see intention-setting becoming a helpful part of your life?

Every insight, big or small, is a step toward living with more clarity, meaning, and presence.

Affirmation This Week

"I am learning to move through my day with clarity, purpose, and intention."

CHAPTER 3

Right Here, Right Now: The Power Of Presence

"Do not dwell in the past, do not dream of the future, concentrate the mind on the present moment."

- Buddha

How often, in the last week, can you say you were fully present in the moment? When was the last time you sat down with no distractions and watched the clouds drift by, or paused to feel the sun on your skin, or focused on your breathing for a moment before moving on to the next task?

This simple practice, pausing and being present, is one of the main techniques I use to help slow my life down. As a working mum juggling the demands of a career, supporting my kids with school and extracurricular activities, and somehow trying to keep everyone in clean clothes and fed (I never knew two teenage boys could eat so much!) I found myself stuck in a cycle of cooking, cleaning, and working with very little space in between. I was often running on empty, too exhausted at the end of my day to do anything for myself.

But when I started to incorporate mindfulness into my life, my mindset and perspective changed dramatically. Instead of feeling as if I was constantly rushing from one thing to the next, those brief, mindful pauses, just a few moments here and there, refreshed and grounded me. They reduced that anxious feeling of being rushed all the time and gave me space to stop, breathe, reconnect, and reset.

Those small, quiet moments became sacred and, for the first time in a long while, I gave myself permission to stop. In those pauses, something profound began to unfold. A deeper sense of connection to something far greater than myself. I found myself noticing and cherishing the simplest things. The way light danced through the trees, the rhythm of my breath, the softness of a morning breeze. Awe crept in gently, and with it came a deeper sense of peace. Even when life felt messy or chaotic, I could return to that stillness. It became my anchor. My safe space.

I started to wonder what's really happening in those pauses? Why did something so simple feel so powerful? That curiosity led me to explore the deeper meaning of mindfulness and presence, not just as abstract concepts, but as everyday practices woven into the life I was already living. I discovered that mindfulness isn't something you have to schedule or prepare for. It's something you can begin right now, in the middle of your day, with nothing but your attention and your senses. It's available at any moment if you choose to pause and tune in.

What It Really Means To Be Present

At its heart, mindfulness is about tuning into your senses, what you can see, hear, feel, smell, and taste. By focusing on the sensory details of a moment, with either one or all of your senses, you shift your awareness out of your head and back into your body, anchoring yourself in the here and now.

When you fully immerse yourself in what you're doing, whether it's eating, washing the dishes, hanging clothes on the line, or simply noticing the warmth of the sun on your skin as you walk from the car to the office, something shifts. Ordinary moments feel richer, more vivid, even comforting. It's as if time slows down, your worries fade into the background, and for a brief, beautiful moment, you're simply alive, grounded in the now.

One of my favourite rituals is walking barefoot through my garden. I pause to notice how the plants have grown, the vibrant colours of the flowers, the layers of green, and the tiny bugs flitting between leaves. Yes, I even talk to my plants and tell them how gorgeous they are, I'm that person!

And in less than ten minutes, I feel grounded and calm. Those few mindful minutes are a small pocket of peace, enough to reset my day and restore my perspective.

What Mindfulness Can Do For You

A growing body of research has confirmed what many ancient traditions have long known. Regular mindfulness can have a powerful, positive effect on your mental, emotional, and even physical health. From stress relief to improved sleep, the benefits are real and accessible to anyone, no matter how busy life is.

Here are some of the ways mindfulness can support your well-being:

- Improves mood and mindset
- Cultivates natural gratitude
- Boosts your connection to yourself, others, and the world around you
- Helps you to see awe in the little things
- Reduces negative thinking by teaching you to observe your thoughts, not get drawn into them
- Enhances emotional regulation and helps you pause before reacting
- Slows down your experience of time, making moments feel fuller, richer, and less rushed
- Creates space for insight and inspiration

Mindfulness vs. Meditation: What's The Difference?

Mindfulness and meditation are often used interchangeably, and while one isn't better than the other, they serve two distinct and useful purposes. Mindfulness is the gentle art of bringing your awareness out of your busy mind and into your body, into the richness of your immediate experience. It's about allowing yourself to be in the moment, to notice what is happening within and around you through your senses and your thoughts, without judgment or commentary. No labelling, no fixing, not good or bad, right or wrong, it just is.

Meditation, on the other hand, is more of an inward journey. It's a quiet turning away from the noise of the outside world and stepping into the inner landscape of your mind, your thoughts, emotions, and deeper consciousness.

Where mindfulness anchors you in the now through your body and senses, meditation invites you to float inward, to explore the vast, still spaces within. One grounds you in presence; the other guides you into depth. Both are pathways to awareness, each with its own benefits and gifts.

How Do I Become Mindful?

Becoming more mindful doesn't mean changing your whole life, it's about changing how you engage with it. You can weave mindful moments into your everyday routine, the life you're already living. You don't need to carve out big blocks of time or have any special equipment to make it happen. Below are some simple, practical ways that are natural, accessible, and surprisingly effective to build mindfulness into your life.

Use Your Senses

As mentioned earlier, your senses help to anchor you in the present moment by giving you something tangible to focus on, which prevents your mind from wandering and being dragged into your thoughts. You can use one of your senses or all of them; it's up to you.

It Can Be Short

Even a few moments of practice here and there can make a meaningful difference. In fact, sprinkling small pockets of mindfulness throughout your day can be as powerful as a single, longer practice, sometimes even more so. What matters most is consistency, not duration.

Use Your Imagination

Anything can be a mindfulness activity; it's only limited by your imagination.

It can be as simple as:
- Taking some deep breaths at your desk.
- Enjoying a song in your car and singing along.
- Being mindful when eating.
- Looking around at nature while on a walk.

Liz Anderson

Turn Daily Tasks Into Mindful Moments

Our days are filled with small, ordinary tasks, the kind we often rush through or do on autopilot. But these everyday moments can become invitations to pause, breathe, and practise mindfulness. Take hanging out the washing, for example. It might seem like just another chore, but I've learned to turn it into a moment of presence. I enjoy the stretch it takes to reach the clothesline (which has to be high so my husband doesn't bump his head every time he walks past!). I feel the warmth of the sun on my skin, a quiet reminder that I'm alive and here. And when I'm finished, I take a moment to look up at the sky, watching the clouds drift and change shape, imagining the different animals they resemble. This simple routine might only take five minutes, but it calms my mind, settles my body, and brings me back to a sense of clarity and control.

Habit Bundling

One of the easiest and most effective ways to build a mindfulness practice is through habit bundling, which is pairing a new, intentional habit with something you already do. Piggybacking a new habit on an old one makes it easier to remember and more natural to sustain.

Take your morning coffee for example, try turning this daily ritual into a mindful moment. Sit with your drink and really immerse yourself in the experience. Notice the rich aroma rising from the cup. Feel the warmth of the mug in your hands. Let the taste linger on your tongue. Is it bold, smooth, earthy, sweet? Tune into the way your body feels as you take that first sip.

Maybe it brings comfort, energy, or even a sense of calm anticipation for the day ahead.

This small shift turns an automatic routine into a grounding ritual. It doesn't take any extra time, just a little extra attention, and these tiny moments of presence start to reshape the rhythm of your day.

Use Online Resources

There are some great apps for mindfulness online, so get searching! When you're starting out, a little structure helps your brain to be more present and increases your confidence in your mindfulness journey.

Mix It Up

Try a few different mindfulness practices and see which ones work best for you personally. Having a range of techniques in your toolkit is especially useful on challenging days. That way, if one doesn't work you have other options to turn to.

Set Reminders

When mindfulness slips away, it's not because we don't care, it's because we go on autopilot and get distracted. Use simple cues to nudge you gently back into the here and now. Pause and reconnect by setting a phone reminder at lunchtime that says, "Take a breath," or a sticky note on your laptop, or even note on your toilet door (although you may not want to take a deep breath in there!).

These small prompts invite you to notice what's happening right now. The rise and fall of your breath, the tension in your shoulders, the taste of your food. Over time, these moments of pausing add up, training your mind to return to presence more naturally, even without the external reminder.

Make It a Routine, Not Just a Rescue

Physical fitness requires regular exercise to keep your body strong and healthy and mental fitness is exactly the same. When you cultivate a steady mindfulness routine, even during calm, uneventful times, you build resilience from the inside out. Because you've developed your mindfulness 'muscles' consistently through the steady times, these techniques and tools have become a natural part of you. They are then immediately available and are far more effective when you need a calm grounding moment. Instead of scrambling into a last-minute, chaotic rescue, you have a steady, soothing refuge at your fingertips that you know works.

I've worked with many clients over the years who try mindfulness only in moments of crisis, often for the first time, and then say, "That didn't work. Mindfulness isn't for me." But when I invite them to practice mindfulness regularly, even when things feel okay, they slowly build a habit. And more often than not, a few weeks later, they notice something remarkable. Not only do the crisis moments feel less frequent, but when challenges do arise, they handle them more skilfully and with less distress than they previously did.

Ten Mindfulness Techniques

Here are ten mindfulness practices to help you slow down and come back to yourself. Some are simple, some playful and others quietly nourishing. Use them as inspiration and see which ones feel natural for you, add them to your toolkit, and make them your own.

1. Mindful Breathing

- Find a comfortable place to sit. Allow your body to settle, and either close your eyes or softly rest your gaze on a spot in the room.
- Begin by bringing your attention to your breath.
- Gentle, natural breathing, in and out.
- Notice the rise and fall of your stomach as you breathe. Feel it gently expanding with each inhale, and softening with each exhale.
- If thoughts drift into your mind, that's perfectly okay. There's no need to judge them or push them away. Simply notice them, and gently guide your focus back to your breath, to the steady rhythm of your belly rising and falling.
- Now, expand your awareness just a little. What sounds can you hear around you? How does your body feel resting in the chair? Can you feel the air on your skin? How does it feel? Is it cool or warm, still or moving?
- Take three slow, deep breaths, feeling the air move in and out of your lungs.

- When you feel ready, gently open your eyes, and return to your day, a little more grounded, a little more present.

2. The 5 4 3 2 1 Method

- What are five things you can see around you that are the colour green? You could change this up and try to find five things the colour blue or five things starting with the letter "B". It can be any colour or any letter.
- What are four things you can touch or feel? Maybe it's the clothes on your skin or how your body feels in the chair or how the air feels on your skin. Notice the sensations in your body. Is it warm or cold, soft or hard, comfortable or uncomfortable?
- What are three things you can hear around you? Do you hear birds, cars, the sound of your breathing, the hum of an air conditioner?
- What are two things you can smell? Take in the scents around you. Do you smell food, flowers or feet? Is it refreshing or not so pleasant?
- What's one thing around you that you can taste? It doesn't have to be food, maybe it's toothpaste or dental floss, maybe it's herbal tea, some gum or maybe it's nothing at all.
- Finish this exercise with three deep breaths.

3. Body Scan Meditation

Sit or lie down comfortably and mentally scan your body from head to toe. Notice any tension or discomfort without judgment. Breathe into those areas and allow them to relax. This exercise helps you connect with your body and release stress.

4. Single-Tasking (Doing One Thing at a Time)

Choose one activity and give it your undivided attention, whether it's eating, folding laundry, or brushing your teeth. Notice every detail, movement, and sensation rather than multitasking or letting your mind wander. Pretend you're an alien and it's the first time you have ever done this activity: approach it with wonder and curiosity.

5. Mindful Eating

Setting the stage

> Get your food ready and arrange it nicely on a special plate. If you need cutlery, use something nice that you wouldn't usually use, like good silverware or chopsticks.
>
> Find a quiet space. Sit comfortably, free from distractions.
>
> Take a few deep breaths. Let your body and mind arrive in the moment.

Seeing

> Look at it as if you've never seen it before.
>
> Observe the shape, texture, colour, and shadows.
>
> "What do I notice visually that I might usually overlook?"

Smelling

    Slowly bring it to your nose and inhale.

    Explore the aroma. Sweet? Earthy? Sharp?

    "What happens in my body or mouth as I smell it?"

Placing

    Take a bite but don't chew yet.

    Notice how your mouth reacts. Do you salivate? Does your tongue move automatically?

Tasting

    Begin to very slowly chew.

    Pay close attention to the flavours, the texture and how it changes.

    Chew longer than you usually would and notice when you instinctively want to swallow.

    "What does it taste like? What layers of flavour can I detect?"

Swallowing

    When you feel ready, swallow.

    Observe the movement as the food goes down your throat.

Reflecting

    How did this feel compared to your usual way of eating?

    Do you feel more satisfied, or more aware?

    "What might change if you ate this way more often?"

You can do this with a single bite at any meal or with a snack. It's a lovely way to reconnect with food and with your body.

6. Do Something Creative

Doing something creative, like drawing, gardening, knitting, baking, or playing music, is a powerful form of mindfulness because it naturally draws you into the present moment. When you're focused on the rhythm of your hands, the texture of materials, or the unfolding of an idea, your mind has less space to ruminate or worry. Creativity engages your senses and attention in a gentle, absorbing way, helping you feel grounded, calm, and connected to yourself. It's not about the end result, it's about being fully present in the process.

7. Start and End Your Day Mindfully

How you begin and close your day sets the tone for everything in between. Before you rise , take a few quiet moments to connect with your mind and body. Focus on your breath, feel your body waking up, slowly stretch and wiggle gently, and set your intentions for the day ahead.

At night, create a mindful ritual to gently close your day. Bring your awareness back to your breath as you lie in bed. Let yourself sink into stillness, releasing the day's tension and calming your mind for restful sleep.

These simple transition points (waking and preparing for rest) shape your whole day more than you might realise. Beginning and ending on a mindful note nurtures calmness, clarity, and intention, enabling you move through life with greater ease and grace.

8. Shower Meditation

Turn your shower into a mindfulness practice. As the water flows over you, imagine it washing away stress and tension. Focus on the temperature, the sound of the water, and how it feels on your skin. It can be a great way to reset your mind.

9. Mindful Listening

Choose a piece of music, a natural soundscape (like ocean waves or birdsong), or simply sit in a space where you can listen to the world around you.

Close your eyes if it feels comfortable, and let your entire focus rest on the sounds.

Notice the rhythm, tone and layers of sound. If it's music, can you hear individual instruments?

If it's your environment, can you pick out distant and close sounds?

Try not to label or analyse, just allow the sound to wash over you and anchor your awareness to the present moment.

When your mind wanders (and it will), gently return to listening.

This practice helps to deepen presence and quiet the mental chatter.

10. Mindful Transitions

Use the moments between the activities in your day as opportunities for mindfulness.

For example, when you switch tasks at work, finish a phone call, park your car, or even when you're waiting for the kettle to boil, pause for just thirty seconds.

Take one or two slow breaths. Notice how your body feels. Have a little stretch.

When you reset rather than rush, you create natural pauses in your day, to refresh, stay centred and intentional rather than reactive.

Mindful Moments All Day Long

Now that you've acquired some techniques to try, you might be wondering, how does this actually fit into a busy day? It can sound like it would take a lot of extra time, but it doesn't have to. To give you a clearer picture, let me walk you through what a mindful day could look like for someone balancing the usual everyday responsibilities.

Morning Routine – Start Your Day with Intention

- **Mindful Breathing (1-2 min):** Before you get out of bed, take a few deep breaths and set an intention for the day. Ask yourself, How do I want to feel today?

- **Mindful Eating (5 min):** Have breakfast without distractions, no scrolling, just focus on the taste, texture, and aroma of your food.

During Work or Daily Tasks – Stay Grounded

- **The Pause & Breathe Rule (15 sec):** Before opening an email or responding to a message, take a deep breath and centre yourself.
- **Single-Tasking (ongoing):** Choose one task to do with full attention, whether it's typing an email, making a phone call, or even washing dishes.
- **The Five Senses Check-In (1 min):** If you feel overwhelmed, stop for a moment and engage all five senses to bring yourself back to the present.

Afternoon Reset – Break the Stress Cycle

- **Grounding with Nature (5-10 min):** Step outside, take a walk, or just sit in the sun. If you're at work, look out the window and notice the sky, trees, or any natural elements.
- **Body Scan Meditation (5 min):** Midway through your day, take a break to check in with your body. Release tension in your shoulders, jaw, or anywhere you feel tightness.

Evening Routine – Wind Down with Presence

- **Shower Meditation (5 min):** Use your evening shower as a time to be present. Feel the warm

water, take deep breaths, and visualise washing away any stress from the day.
- **Digital Detox Moment (10-15 min):** Before bed, put your phone away and spend time journaling, stretching, or simply sitting in silence.
- **Mindful Breathing (2-3 min):** As you lie in bed, take a few slow, deep breaths to calm your nervous system and prepare for restful sleep.

As you can see, mindfulness doesn't require large blocks of time or dramatic changes to your routine. Even weaving in just one or two of the simple practices mentioned above can shift the pace of your day making it feel slower and calmer.

Heartbeat Of The Chapter

Hopefully, this chapter has helped you understand what mindfulness is, how it might benefit you, and how you can start to add it into your life in ways that are natural and doable for you.

It's the small moments, where we take the time to pause and connect with ourselves and the world, where we become observers, observers of our thoughts and emotions, not with judgment but with a curiosity that allows us the space to detach from unhelpful thinking and the busyness of life, recalibrate and move forward with a positive, empowered and calm mindset.

Challenge This Week

Choose a few different mindfulness techniques to explore this week. Try to do one every day if possible. If you're looking for more inspiration, head online. There's a wealth of great resources, ideas, and mindfulness apps available. Have a browse and see what sparks your interest.

At the end of the week, reflect on how the practices made you feel.

- How did you feel while doing the mindfulness exercises?
- Did you find it easy or hard to be in the moment?
- Did it give you a greater sense of calm and peace?
- Is it something you can see yourself continuing with?

Write down what your favourite mindfulness exercises are.

Affirmation This Week

"I am learning to become more mindful in my daily life and even small moments of stillness nourish me."

CHAPTER 4

Everyday Grace: Finding Joy & Gratitude In The Ordinary

"Enjoy the little things, for one day you may look back and realise they were the big things."

- Robert Brault

A few years ago, I decided to do a free three-month trial subscription to a news service. It was just after COVID emerged, and many of my clients were worried about the state of the world and wanted to discuss what was happening, so I thought it would be a good idea to stay up to date with current events.

Great idea, right? Straight away, I started receiving notifications about local and world events, and I'll admit, I became a little obsessive about checking the news. At first, I felt well-informed and intelligent (I mean, smart people read the news, right?). It wasn't long, however, before the constant bombardment of negative and fear-inducing stories bore down on me, making me feel anxious and hopeless about life. I found myself thinking about news stories in the middle of the night, worrying about the future my kids would be walking into and focusing more on what I didn't have than what I did. It took a toll on me, not just mentally but physically. I was exhausted, having broken sleep, getting sick more often, and constantly on edge. My mind was always racing, and I felt foggy, irritable and stuck in my own head.

When my free trial was over, I decided to cancel the subscription. I realised I was stuck in a negative mindset and needed to do something to turn it around. I'd witnessed many of my clients shift from a negative to a positive mindset over the years, and almost every one of them had developed a regular gratitude practice as an essential part of that shift. So, I decided I'd do that too.

Each morning, and again before bed, I began a small ritual of naming three things I was grateful for. At first, it felt awkward, almost forced. My mind seemed wired to notice what was missing rather than what was present. But over time, the practice became easier, almost effortless.

I noticed a shift inside me. Instead of letting feelings of lack or negativity take over, I found myself able to move through those emotions more quickly. I could see both sides, the struggles yes, but also the small glimmers of hope that had always been there, waiting to be noticed.

I realised that, while I couldn't control everything in life, I could choose where to place my attention. And when I chose gratitude, I discovered how much I really did have to be thankful for. That simple practice left me feeling lighter, calmer, and, for the first time in a long while, at peace. Gratitude has now become a steady, uplifting presence in my life, enriching my daily experience and reminding me that even in difficult times, there is always something worth noticing.

What Is Gratitude?

Gratitude is the practice of noticing and appreciating what brings meaning and joy, no matter how small, even in the midst of life's messiness. It's that feeling of thankfulness, whether for something big, like a life-changing event, or something simple, like a warm cup of coffee or sunlight streaming through the window. Gratitude shifts our focus away from what's not working or weighing us down towards what is steady, supportive, and life-affirming. We become more present and grounded, moving from a sense of lack to one of connection and possibility.

Gratitude can rewire our brain, guiding it away from negativity and pessimism toward a more balanced and hopeful perspective. When we dwell only on what's wrong, it can amplify anxiety and fear, pulling us into hopelessness. But when we notice even the smallest sources of comfort or beauty, it is as if the clouds have parted and the light has broken through, revealing that we have more to be thankful for than we first imagined.

Although gratitude can sound vague or overly sentimental, research in the field of positive psychology shows otherwise. Countless studies confirm that cultivating gratitude reduces stress and anxiety, strengthens emotional resilience, and fosters a deeper sense of purpose, connection, and even awe in everyday life.

Three Key Aspects of Gratitude

Gratitude may seem like a single practice, but actually it has layers. To really experience its benefits, it helps to think of it as a process with three interconnected parts: awareness, appreciation, and expression. Each part plays an important role in deepening how we connect with life's big and small moments.

Awareness

Awareness is the point where gratitude ties into mindfulness. You can't appreciate what you don't notice, and you can't notice what you don't take the time to observe. When we slow down, our awareness sharpens, and we are able to catch the little details that so often slip by, like the taste of a decadent piece of cake, the smell of freshly cut grass, a warm smile from a stranger, or the simple beauty of flowers blooming in the garden. These moments matter. They ground us, lift us, and draw us back into the present.

Appreciation

Noticing something is the first step, but allowing yourself to value it is where gratitude deepens. Appreciation means pausing long enough to let the moment land, to feel its significance instead of brushing past it. It's the difference between glancing at the sunset or stopping to gaze at it, letting its colours sink in. Between sipping your morning coffee while distracted or truly savouring that first warm mouthful. Appreciation invites us to stop taking the ordinary for granted and recognise it as extraordinary in its own way.

Expression

Finally, gratitude becomes even more powerful when we give it voice. This can be as simple as a silent "thank you" in your mind, writing in a journal, or telling someone directly how much they mean to you. Expression reinforces the feeling of gratitude, both for ourselves and others. It shifts our perspective from lack to abundance and strengthens our connections, making gratitude not just an internal practice but a shared one.

What If I Can't Find Anything To Be Grateful For?

I get it, when life is going smoothly, gratitude feels natural and comes easily. But when everything feels heavy and hard, it can be almost impossible to find anything worth appreciating. And let's be honest, gratitude is not the right response in every situation. It has its time and place.

The pressure to always maintain a positive mindset can lead us into the trap of toxic positivity, the belief that only good vibes are acceptable, and that any difficult feelings should be pushed aside. This way of thinking can leave us feeling guilty or ashamed of our emotions, or pressured to put on a grateful smile while quietly struggling inside. Worse still, it can minimise and dismiss the very real pain that we, or others, might be going through.

Gratitude doesn't mean denying our struggles or pretending everything's fine. Instead, it invites us to acknowledge what's hard while still allowing space for even the smallest glimmers of support, beauty, or comfort. It's not about being grateful for the hardship itself, but about finding little anchors of hope that help us move through it.

So when life is tough and you're struggling to find something to be grateful for:

Start Small—Really Small

Look for tiny, grounding things, a warm drink, a breath of fresh air, a kind text, a moment of quiet. You're not trying to pretend you're okay; you are bringing your awareness to the small things around you that can alleviate the pain and provide comfort.

Change the Question

Instead of asking, "What can I be grateful for?" try asking, "What hasn't completely fallen apart?" or "What's helping me survive this moment?" It's a softer entry point when gratitude feels out of reach.

Acknowledge the Hard Stuff First

Gratitude isn't a bypass; it's a companion. Before trying to find something to be thankful for, say what hurts first. Sometimes, simply being honest about how you're feeling is the first step towards healing. From that place of truth, a sense of appreciation for your own resilience or the support of a friend might come naturally.

Once we've given ourselves permission to be real about what hurts, we can also notice the small things that are nourishing or uplifting us. Which brings us to...

Can Noticing The Little Things Really Make A Difference?

Gratitude and thankfulness aren't reserved only for the big, obvious moments like when someone does something kind for us, or we achieve something significant. When we pause to appreciate the small beauties around us, a flower blooming through a crack in the pavement, the comfort of a heartfelt hug, we are turning these moments into mindful experiences.

These little instances not only enrich our day, they also let gratitude grow naturally, organically, without having to force it. In recognising these small moments of beauty, we are connecting with something greater than ourselves. This is where spirituality can come in and enrich our experience of gratitude even further.

Spirituality used to be underrated and viewed as relatively unimportant by many health professionals. Nowadays, this assessment has altered dramatically. More and more, spirituality has moved into the spotlight as an integral part of the human experience and one that can play a significant role in an individual's overall physical and mental well-being. Spirituality is a deeply personal and individual experience. It helps us make sense of the world and our place in it, offering a guiding philosophy to live by and a sense of meaning that steadies us through life's ups and downs.

Some people connect with spirituality through prayer or religious traditions; others find it in meditation, yoga, creativity, or simply by being in nature. There's no single right way or path, it's as unique as you are. When woven into the practice of gratitude, spirituality deepens our sense of appreciation and broadens our perspective. In today's fast-paced, uncertain world, that connection can be a much-needed source of comfort and hope.

Simple Ways To Add Gratitude Into Your Day

When, life is already full to overflowing, the idea of adding another thing to your day can be daunting, even overwhelming. But like mindfulness, practising gratitude doesn't have to be time-consuming or complicated. Even the smallest moments of appreciation will change how you feel and move through your day.

Below are some simple ideas to help you weave gratitude into your life in ways that are natural and achievable.

Daily Gratitude Practices

- **Add a little joy activity into every day** – It can be a small activity like watering the garden, watching the sunrise or sunset, brewing your favourite tea, or going for a swim.
- **Gratitude Journal** – Each day, write down three things you're grateful for. They don't have to be big; simple things like a good cup of coffee, a kind word from a friend, or a beautiful picture can make a difference.
- **Morning Gratitude** – Before you even get out of bed, take a moment to think of one thing you're grateful for and carry that feeling into your day.
- **Gratitude Jar** – Keep a jar where you write down things you're grateful for on small slips of paper. Over time, it becomes a visual reminder of all the

little joys in your life. You can read them whenever you need a boost.

- **Gratitude Walk** – Go for a short walk and actively notice things you appreciate, nature, fresh air, the sounds around you. Focusing on the beauty of the present moment can help cultivate gratitude.
- **Express Gratitude to Others** – Send a heartfelt text, write a letter, or simply tell someone how much you appreciate them. Expressing gratitude strengthens relationships and spreads positivity.
- **Gratitude Round at Dinner** – Go around the table and have each family member share one thing they're grateful for that day. This fosters positive conversations and helps everyone appreciate the small joys in life.
- **Gratitude Bedtime Routine** – Before bedtime, ask your kids (or each other) to share one thing they loved about their day. It's a great way to end the day on a positive note and encourage reflection.
- **Family Gratitude Journal** – Keep a shared gratitude journal where each family member can write (or draw) something they're thankful for. Over time, it becomes a beautiful keepsake of happy memories.
- **Gratitude Sticky Notes** – Have a gratitude wall or a whiteboard where family members can post sticky notes with things they appreciate about their day or each other.

Mindfulness-Based Gratitude Practices

- **Gratitude Meditation** – Sit quietly, focus on your breath, and bring to mind things, people, or experiences you're grateful for. Let the feelings of appreciation fill your heart.

- **Grateful Eating** – Before eating, take a moment to appreciate your meal, the flavours, the effort that went into making it, and how it nourishes your body.
- **Gratitude Breathing** – With each inhale, think of something or someone you're thankful for. With each exhale, imagine sending gratitude out into the world.

Deeper Reflection Gratitude Practices

- **Weekly Reflection** – At the end of the week, reflect on what went well and what you're grateful for. This helps you focus on the positives rather than what went wrong.
- **Reframing Challenges with Gratitude** – When faced with difficulties, ask yourself: What lesson can I learn from this? Or is there something positive that has come out of this situation? This doesn't mean ignoring struggles or minimising their impact on you, but having a growth mindset means you can recognise growth opportunities when they present themselves.

Seasonal & Special Gratitude Practices

- **Gratitude Countdown** – Create a gratitude countdown where each day leading up to a holiday or special event family members share something they're thankful for.

- **Acts of Kindness Together** – Show gratitude by giving back. Volunteer together, donate toys or clothes, or do small acts of kindness like baking cookies for a neighbour.

Practical Exercises: Experiencing Gratitude in Action

Instead of just thinking about gratitude, let's bring it to life with small, tangible actions. Pick one or more of these exercises and try them today:

The 5-Minute Gratitude Hunt

- Take a walk around your home, garden, or neighbourhood.
- Notice five small things that bring you a sense of appreciation – a flower, a sound, a smell, a texture, or a sight.
- Write them down or take a photo to capture the moment.

Micro-Moments of Gratitude

- Set a timer for three times throughout today.
- Pause for thirty seconds each time and notice one thing you appreciate in the moment.
- Take a deep breath in as you acknowledge it, letting it fill your awareness.

Mindful Gratitude Bite

- Choose one simple daily activity like drinking coffee, washing dishes, or walking to your car.
- Slow down and fully notice it. Think: "In this moment, what am I grateful for?"
- Transform ordinary mundane tasks or situations into moments of awareness and appreciation.

Heartbeat Of The Chapter

Gratitude has a way of shifting our perspective, from what's lacking or overwhelming to what's meaningful and worth appreciating. It's not about denying pain or pretending everything is fine. Instead, it helps us to hold both truths. The hard and the hopeful. In a world that moves fast and often feels too much, gratitude offers a way to slow down. It soothes the nervous system, quiets the mental noise, and draws us back to the richness of the present moment. It reminds us that even life's simplest moments, when noticed, can be deeply nourishing and bring richness to our soul.

Challenge This Week

This week, pick a couple of gratitude ideas from this chapter and commit to exploring them for a week. Each day, spend a few minutes intentionally practising gratitude. Then, check in with yourself at the end of the week:

- How did it feel to pause and notice something to appreciate?
- Did certain exercises feel easier or more enjoyable than others?
- Did this practice help you feel more present, calmer, or connected?

Optional twist: Give yourself a theme for each day, like nature, relationships, comfort, creativity, movement, or moments of joy. This keeps it playful and makes noticing easier.

Affirmation This Week

"Each day offers something to be thankful for, and I choose to see it."

CHAPTER 5

Self-Care: The Art of Looking After You

> *"Caring for myself is not self-indulgence, it is self-preservation."*
>
> - Audre Lorde

I absolutely love bubble baths. In fact, being immersed in water, of any kind, is my true happy place. I'm convinced I must have been a dolphin in a past life because I find so much peace in the water. The sensation of it on my skin, the weightlessness, and that carefree feeling. I feel all my stress melt away, and time seems to stand still. Being in water is one of my many joyful rituals, the little practices I embrace to fill my cup, recharge, and reset.

Self-care has always been a big part of my life. As a psychologist, it's been ingrained in me from the very beginning: at university, in government roles, and in private practice, the message has always been clear. Self-care is essential if you want to manage your mental health successfully, especially when your work involves helping others with theirs.

But the truth is, self-care isn't just for therapists or people in helping professions. No matter what season of life you're in, whether you're working, retired, raising a family, or living on your own, self-care matters just as much for you too.

Creating rituals that nourish you doesn't just restore your energy; it resets your mindset and builds the emotional resilience you need to face the tough days. When you take time to care for yourself in ways that are meaningful, you're not being selfish, you're laying the foundation for a healthier, more balanced life. (And honestly, you're usually much more pleasant to be around as a result!)

Self-Care Isn't Selfish. Here's Why

Self-care is often misunderstood as an indulgence or a selfish act. In reality, it's a necessity. Taking care of yourself isn't about being self-centred; it's about making sure you're physically, emotionally, and mentally nourished so you can show up as your best self, for you and for those around you. Just as you can't pour from an empty cup, you can't give your best energy, love, or attention if you are running on empty. When you prioritise self-care, you're really investing in your ability to be present, grounded, and emotionally resilient.

Think about it, you're probably great at making sure your loved ones feel valued, heard, and cared for. But how often do you give that same level of care to yourself? If you're constantly stretched too thin, juggling a million things, and ignoring your own needs, it's only a matter of time before resentment creeps in and you feel frustrated, exhausted, and ready to snap.

The good news is, self-care doesn't have to be complicated or look the same for everyone. What works for me might not work for you, and that's perfectly fine. It's about finding what helps you reset and recharge, even if it's only for a few minutes. The key is carving out time to focus on yourself, preferably without interruptions or distractions. It could be a walk, reading a book, journaling, or yes... sinking into a bubble bath.

I know arranging self-care can be tough with kids who seem to have an uncanny knack for sensing the exact moment you want some alone time and deciding that's when they need your full attention. But the more we gently help them understand that everyone needs their own space to feel calmer and happier, the more they'll adjust to the idea. (Also, in my experience, a well-timed chocolate bribe doesn't hurt either!)

Talking About Self-Care With Sceptics

Not everyone understands the importance of self-care. Some may see it as selfish, unnecessary, or even a sign of weakness, especially in cultures or environments that glorify busyness and self-sacrifice. If you find yourself trying to explain self-care to someone who doesn't support or prioritise it, here are some ways to communicate your perspective effectively.

Shift the Narrative: It's about Sustainability, not Indulgence

If someone sees self-care as unnecessary, reframe the conversation by emphasising that self-care is about sustainability, not selfishness. **You might say:**

"Self-care isn't about avoiding responsibilities. It's about making sure I have the energy to handle them well. When I take time to recharge, I can be more present, more productive, and more engaged in life."

For those who value hard work and productivity, it may help to explain that burnout and exhaustion actually make people less effective. Taking breaks, resting, and caring for yourself leads to better outcomes and long-term success.

Use the Oxygen Mask Analogy

A great way to illustrate the necessity of self-care is by referencing the aeroplane oxygen mask analogy:

"You know how on aeroplanes, they tell you to put on your own oxygen mask before helping others? That's because if you pass out, you're no help to anyone. The same applies to life. If I don't take care of myself, I can't show up fully for others."

This analogy is relatable and reinforces the idea that self-care isn't selfish, it's responsible.

Emphasise the Impact on Others

If someone doesn't see self-care as important, they might be more open to hearing about how it benefits those around you. When you take care of yourself, you:

- Have more patience and kindness in relationships
- Can support others more effectively
- Model healthy habits for family and friends

You could say:

"When I take time to care for myself, I'm in a better mood, more patient, and less stressed. That means I can be a better partner/friend/parent/colleague."

If they still resist the idea, ask them to reflect:

"Would you want me to always feel exhausted, frustrated, or drained? Taking care of myself helps prevent that."

Address Guilt and Cultural Expectations

Some people have been brought up to believe that self-sacrifice equals love or that rest must be earned. **If this is the case, gently challenge that belief:**

"Taking care of myself doesn't mean I don't care about others. It means I'm making sure I can be there for them in the best way possible."

For parents, caregivers, or workaholics, remind them that self-care is also a form of self-respect:

"If I neglect myself, I'm teaching others that it's okay to ignore their own needs. I want to show that taking care of yourself is a healthy, normal part of life."

Lead by Example

Sometimes, the best way to communicate the value of self-care is to embody it yourself. Instead of arguing, simply show the benefits through your own actions. As you become more balanced, energised, and present, those who once dismissed self-care may start to notice the difference and even become curious about it themselves.

You can also invite them to participate in self-care with you:

"Why don't we take a break and go for a walk together?"

"Let's have a quiet night in and enjoy some good food without distractions."

By making it a shared experience, you help them ease into the idea of self-care without resistance.

It's Okay If They Don't Understand

Not everyone will immediately embrace the idea of self-care, and that's okay. You don't need validation from others to prioritise your well-being. Stay firm in your boundaries, continue practising self-care unapologetically, and know that taking care of yourself is a personal choice, not something that requires anyone else's approval.

If someone still doesn't understand, simply say:

"I respect your perspective, but I've found that self-care helps me be my best self. This is something that's important to me."

By standing up for your needs with confidence, you reinforce the message that self-care is not negotiable; it's essential.

40 Self-Care Practices To Nourish Your Mind, Body And Soul

Often, when I talk to clients about self-care and ask what helps them feel relaxed, recharged, or nurtured, they'll name one or two things, then look at me quizzically, as if I've asked them to solve a complex math problem, before shrugging their shoulders. For many, self-care feels like a foreign concept, something they might occasionally indulge in but rarely practice regularly. So if you find yourself struggling to think of ideas, I've included a list of 40 self-care activities below to help spark inspiration.

For the Body

1. Take a warm bath or shower.
2. Go for a walk in nature.
3. Stretch or do gentle yoga.
4. Do some exercise, go to the gym.
5. Dance to your favourite music.
6. Get a massage (or try a self-massage tool).
7. Prepare and enjoy a nourishing meal.
8. Have a sauna.
9. Take a nap without guilt.
10. Get a good night's sleep.
11. Try a new form of movement (Pilates, swimming, tai chi, etc.).

For the Mind

12. Read a book.
13. Listen to a podcast that inspires you.
14. Watch a documentary or educational video.
15. Do a puzzle or play a brain game.
16. Learn something new (a language, instrument, skill).

For the Soul

17. Meditate, even if it's only for five minutes.
18. Spend time in silence or stillness.
19. Watch a sunrise or sunset.

20. Light a candle and sit quietly.
21. Do something creative (draw, paint, write, etc.).
22. Connect with someone you love.
23. Practice deep breathing or grounding techniques.
24. Create a vision board or mood board.
25. Visit a place that makes you feel peaceful.
26. Look through old photos.

Everyday Pleasures

27. Drink your favourite tea or coffee slowly.
28. Wear clothes that feel good on your body.
29. Sit in the sun for a few minutes.
30. Watch a funny movie or show.
31. Bake something from scratch.
32. Tend to houseplants or your garden.
33. Snuggle or play with a pet.
34. Revisit a favourite childhood activity (colouring, board games).

Intentional Self-Care

35. Schedule a day off just for rest.
36. Reflect on your goals or intentions.
37. Write a letter to your future self.
38. Plan a mini retreat or a "do nothing" day.
39. Celebrate something you've accomplished (big or small).
40. Talk to a therapist, coach, or supportive friend.

Practical Exercise: Making Your Own Self-Care Menu

Now that your inspiration has been sparked from the above list, let's create your own self-care menu. This will be your personal toolkit, something you can turn to on those foggy days when it feels hard to think clearly and you're not sure what you need. Having a ready-made list of nourishing ideas on hand makes it easier to take positive action instead of staying stuck or falling into unhelpful habits.

As you create your menu, stay curious. Try different things, mix it up, and think about what might feel calming, energising, or uplifting. Aim for variety. Include some quick and easy practices that you can do at home, and others that get you out into the world when you need a change of scenery. Let's get started!

Step 1 Brainstorm

Find a quiet space where you can think without distractions. Grab a pen and paper, this is where some good old-fashioned brainstorming comes in. Start writing down anything and everything that sounds even remotely soothing, enjoyable or meaningful to you. Don't filter or overthink it, just let the ideas flow. Think about activities that help you feel calm, connected, joyful, creative, or simply cared for.

If you're stuck ask yourself:
- What makes you feel calm or grounded?
- What helps you feel energised or joyful?

- What are your favourite things to do?
- What small things help you feel more like yourself?

Step 2 Group your ideas

Once you have a good list, organise your self-care ideas into a few categories, any ones you like. For example:
- For the body
- For the mind
- For the soul
- At home
- Out of home

Step 3 Make it visible

Write or type out your self-care menu and keep it somewhere visible, on a card, in your journal, on your fridge, or by your bed. The more often you see it, the more likely you are to actually use it, especially on the days you need it most.

Want to make it a little more fun? Jot each idea on a separate slip of paper and pop them into a fancy jar, box or container. When you're feeling low, tired, or just need a little inspiration, pull one out and let it guide your next small act of self-care.

Step 4 Use it often

Refer back to your self-care menu anytime you feel off-balance, need a reset or just need some inspiration. Over time, you'll refine it and discover which practices are most beneficial for you, and hopefully, your list will grow longer over time. So, relax and enjoy!

Heartbeat Of The Chapter

Self-care isn't a luxury; it's a lifeline. It's not about indulgence, it's about balance, honouring your needs, and tending to your soul with the same compassion you so readily show others.

In a world that constantly urges us to do more, achieve more, and be more, self-care becomes a quiet but powerful declaration that you matter. It's the way you pause, notice when your energy is fading, and lovingly offer yourself what you need before burnout takes hold.

You don't have to earn your rest. You are worthy of care simply because you exist. When you allow yourself that care, without guilt or apology, you feel calmer, happier, and more resilient in the face of life's ups and downs.

Self-care is not selfish. It's the foundation that allows you to show up as your best self for your loved ones, your work and most importantly, for you.

Challenge This Week

For the next seven days, carve out ten minutes each day to do one thing that recharges you. You can do longer, but try to do at least ten minutes.

- Choose a time of day that works for you. Morning, lunch break, right before bed, whatever fits into your routine.
- Pick one small self-care activity from the list in this chapter or your own self-care menu.
- Be fully present. No multitasking. No guilt. Just ten intentional minutes that belong to you. Set a timer if you need to.

At the end of the week, reflect on what you noticed:

- Did doing some self-care improve your mood, energy, or focus?
- Did it make your week feel calmer and slower?

The goal is to show yourself that you can make space for your own care, even in small ways.

Affirmation This Week

"I am learning to rest and to nourish my body, mind and soul. Taking care of myself is how I build a strong foundation for everything else."

CHAPTER 6

Simplify, Unclutter & Thrive

"The ability to simplify means to eliminate the unnecessary, so that the necessary may speak."

- Hans Hofmann

Staying on top of housework is hard! You know what I mean, a ton of clean clothes piled on the couch waiting to be folded, a mountain of dirty laundry that never seems to shrink, dog hair magically reappearing on the floor seconds after you've vacuumed, and all the random stuff piling up on the dining room table that you never quite get the time to put away.

Over the years, I've noticed that my environment has a huge impact on how settled I feel. When the house is messy or chaotic, I feel that way inside too, overwhelmed, restless and distracted. But when my space feels clear and under control, it's like my brain follows suit. A calmness washes over me, and I can think more clearly, breathe a little easier, and actually enjoy being in my own home.

Over the years, I've worked hard to create routines and systems that keep the house running smoothly without driving everyone (myself included) crazy. I've simplified wherever I can, not in a perfectionist "everything must be spotless" way, but in a way that feels doable and sustainable for all of us. A couple of times a year, I'll do a bigger spring clean to remove any physical clutter and reorganise what's messy again (hello linen cupboard!). And what's surprised me most about this process was the more simplified and organised my home and life became, the more space and energy I had for the things I actually wanted to do.

But simplifying isn't about having less for the sake of it or striving for a picture-perfect home. Trust me, there's a permanent pile of clean clothes on my couch most days (who knew two teenage boys could go through so many outfits? At least I know they're showering!). Simplifying is really about clearing out the clutter, the physical and the mental, so you can cut down on the distractions and time-wasters to create more space for what's important to you. So why, if it sounds so good, is it often so hard to do?

Liz Anderson

Why Enough Never Feels Like Enough

We live in a world that constantly bombards us with noise, social media, advertising, and the relentless pressure to do more, be more, and buy more. Everywhere we turn, we're told that happiness is just one more thing away. One more purchase. One more goal. One more shiny new gadget, productivity hack, or miracle pill. The message is loud and clear: if you just get this thing, follow that trend, hit that milestone, you will finally feel good. Then life will be amazing!

But here's the truth: that chase never ends.

It's exhausting, isn't it? The endless striving to keep up, to measure up, to present a perfectly curated life, when deep down, all we really crave is a little peace. Yet while we run ourselves ragged buying more, collecting more, chasing after happiness, the simple joys we once cherished slip away. Things like cooking a homemade meal, curling up with a good book, or simply being present with the people we love begin to feel complicated, forced, even laced with guilt.

For me, simplifying isn't just about clearing my environment; it's about stepping away from the cycle of more and choosing fewer but more meaningful experiences. By lightening the load with fewer purchases, fewer commitments, and fewer distractions, I've actually gained more, more calm, more joy, more freedom, and more time. Simplicity hasn't been boring; it's opened space for deeper experiences and genuine connections. It's the guiding principle of quality over quantity.

It's so easy to fall into overcommitting, overbuying, and the fear of missing out. Our lives become so crammed with stuff, both physical and emotional, that we lose the breathing room to notice what we truly enjoy.

Simplifying and decluttering gives us that breathing room back. It strips away the noise and distractions, creating the space to rediscover joy. Simplicity, at its heart, is freedom.

Why Simplify My Life?

Maybe you're wondering, "Okay, sounds good in theory but why go to all this effort? Why does simplifying matter so much?" It's a fair question. After all, it's easy to fall into the trap of thinking, *I'll do it when I have more time, more energy, when life finally settles down*. But the truth is, that perfect moment rarely arrives. Life doesn't simplify itself; you have to choose to make it simpler. And when you do, the rewards are worth it.

Here are a few powerful reasons to start simplifying:

You Reclaim Your Time and Energy

Instead of pouring yourself into endless chores, shopping, or commitments, you free up more time for rest, joy, and the people who matter most.

You Make Decisions With Less Stress

When your life has fewer moving parts, there are fewer choices to agonise over. That means less decision fatigue, less second-guessing, and more clarity about what really matters.

You Create More Space For Creativity and Joy

When your mind isn't cluttered with to-dos and distractions, you notice ideas and opportunities you might have missed. Simplifying often sparks more playfulness, curiosity, and inspiration.

Your Relationships Improve

Less clutter and chaos mean fewer arguments about stuff and schedules. It also means you're more present with loved ones, instead of being distracted or rushing through time together.

You Align Your Life With Your Values

By clearing out what no longer serves you, whether physical possessions, energy-draining commitments, or outdated habits, you make room for the things that reflect who you are and what you care about most.

I'm Convinced! So Where Do I Start?

Clutter isn't just about the piles on your countertops, it sneaks into your schedule, your work life, and even your finances. And the more crowded life feels, the harder it is to slow down and live with intention. The good news is, you don't have to tackle everything at once. In the next section, we'll explore some common areas that tend to get overwhelmed, along with simple, practical ideas you can use to start decluttering those areas.

Decluttering Your Physical Space

Your environment has a direct impact on how you feel. A cluttered home adds stress, while a simplified space makes it easier to breathe and focus. So how do you declutter without doing a full-blown spring clean?

Start Small

Don't try to tackle your whole house in one weekend. Start with one drawer or one shelf. Small wins build momentum.

Use The "One Touch" Rule

When you pick something up, make a decision about it then and there; don't put it back down to deal with later. Decide: keep, toss, donate, or relocate.

The Box Test

Put the items you're unsure about in a box. Seal it, label it with a date (for example, three or six months later), and store it out of sight. If you haven't needed or missed anything in that time, donate the whole box without reopening it.

Declutter by Category (KonMari-style by Marie Kondo)

Choose a category (for example, clothes, books, kitchenware), gather all items in that category from around the house, and go through them one by one, only keeping what you actually use or love. Seeing the full volume of what you own helps you make clearer decisions.

Create a Donation Station

Set up a box or bag somewhere accessible where you can regularly drop things you no longer use. Once it's full, donate it. Repeat.

Ditch the Guilt Clutter

That book you should read but haven't touched in two years? The gift you feel obligated to keep? If it doesn't serve or uplift you, it's okay to let it go.

Give Everything a Home

If it doesn't have a place, it becomes clutter. Assign everything you keep a home and make it a habit to return it there. This saves me a bunch of time because I don't spend hours looking for things!

Declutter with Your Real Lifestyle in Mind

Keep only what supports the way you actually live, not your fantasy self who hosts dinner parties weekly and does yoga every morning at sunrise.

Use the Two-Year Rule

If you haven't used it in a couple of years, consider donating or selling it. Adopt a minimalist mindset. If it's not being used, it's taking up space. If you can't let it go, put it in a box in your garage or shed.

The Surface Sweep

Choose one surface (coffee table, kitchen counter, bathroom vanity). Clear everything off, give it a quick wipe, and only put back the essentials. Visual clutter increases stress. This technique creates instant calm and helps you maintain a more peaceful atmosphere in your home.

Keep What Adds Value or Brings Joy to Your Life

The goal is to surround yourself with things that support your lifestyle and uplift your energy, not objects that just take up space or drain you. If it's not adding value to your present, it's taking up space in your future.

Simplify Your Daily Routine

When your routine is cluttered, even small tasks feel overwhelming. Simplifying how you move through the day brings more ease, flow, and focus.

Pick Three Key Tasks to Focus on Each Day

When everything feels urgent, nothing gets done well. Instead of trying to tackle a mountain of tasks, choose a limited number of priorities for the day. Pick things that, when completed, will move you closer towards your goals. This simple shift helps you stay focused, avoid burnout, and feel productive. If you have something challenging or unpleasant on your list, aim to get it out of the way early. I've found that focusing on the relief I'll feel afterwards makes it easier to push through and get it done.

Try Single-Tasking for Better Results and Less Stress

As we touched on in the chapter about mindfulness, there's real power in doing one thing at a time. When you give a task your full attention, you not only finish faster, but you also make fewer mistakes and feel less overwhelmed. Single-tasking is both mindful and practical. Do one thing, give it your best, then move on. You may be surprised at how much lighter and calmer your day feels as a result.

Meal Plan to Reduce Stress Around Food Decisions

Decision fatigue is real, and nothing drains the joy from an evening faster than the dreaded "What's for dinner?" For the longest time, my first thought when I woke up was, "What on earth am I going to make for dinner tonight?" But once I started doing some simple meal planning and prepping, nothing too extreme, my mornings (and evenings) felt so much lighter and I had more time for other things as well.

Set Reminders

Yes, it's another reminder but this one is about using your tech to take the pressure off your brain. Bills, appointments, errands, even birthdays, handing these over to your phone is like passing the mental load to a reliable assistant. I also keep a weekly planner on my fridge where I write everything down. Having it right in front of me not only jogs my memory when the phone alone isn't enough, it also gives me a clear view of my week so I can mentally prepare for what's coming. I still put everything in my calendar too, because it's not only about remembering, it's about already having time set aside to do things. No more last-minute rushing or forgotten to-dos, just a calmer, more relaxed day.

Streamline Your Work Life

Time is your most valuable resource at work, yet it's also the easiest to waste. By streamlining your days, you'll work more efficiently, get more done, and feel less stressed.

Set Boundaries

Protecting your time at work is just as important as protecting it at home. That might mean saying no to unnecessary meetings, projects that don't align with your priorities, or interruptions that pull you away from focused work. Remember, every "yes" comes at the cost of your attention, energy, or well-being. We'll explore boundaries more deeply in a later chapter, looking at how they can support you at work and in every area of your life.

Batch Tasks

Instead of jumping between emails, calls, and reports all day, try to group similar tasks together. For example, check emails at set times rather than constantly, or dedicate a block of time for administrative work. Batching reduces the energy drain of constant context-switching and reduces brain fatigue.

Use Tech Wisely

Let technology take some of the load off. Use project management tools, shared calendars, and reminders to stay organised and keep tasks visible. Automate repetitive tasks where possible so you can focus on work that genuinely requires your attention.

Declutter Your Environment

A cluttered workspace creates a cluttered mind. Keep your desk clear, tidy up your desktop and shared drives, and make sure files are easy to find. If you have influence in your workplace, encourage uncluttered shared spaces too, like a calm, inviting lunchroom or break area where people can recharge. Even small shifts in the physical environment can reduce stress and boost focus.

Reduce Financial Complexity

Few things weigh us down the way financial stresses do. Simplifying your approach to money can bring a sense of calmness and control, opening the door to greater freedom and peace of mind.

Go Paperless Where You Can

Digitise what matters. Scan and safely back up important documents, then let go of the rest by shredding and recycling. Consider switching to digital billing to cut down on paper clutter. Fewer stacks of paper on your countertops means your mind is clearer and calmer.

Downsize Unnecessary Subscriptions or Services.

Subscriptions are sneaky and can pile up in the background if we're not paying attention. Take some time to review your bank statements, or do a subscription audit to uncover what you are paying for and not using. Do you really need four streaming platforms? A gym membership you never use? Cancel anything that doesn't add value to your life. You'll save money and mental space.

Once I've finished watching a particular show on a streaming platform, I cancel my subscription and only restart it when there's something new I want to see. That way, I'm actually getting value for my money instead of paying for something I'm not using.

Unsubscribe from Marketing Emails

Seriously, one of the most underrated ways to simplify your financial life is to remove temptation. Marketing emails are designed to get you to buy things you didn't know you needed five minutes ago. Unsubscribe, declutter your inbox, and reduce impulse spending in one go. Most marketing emails have an unsubscribe option right at the bottom of the email (usually in the smallest print possible!).

Spring Clean Your Social Media Feeds

Research shows a strong link between excessive social media use and lower self-esteem. Unfollow or mute accounts that leave you feeling drained, not good enough, or caught in comparison mode. Instead, fill your feed with content that makes you smile, laugh, feel inspired, or connected. Prioritise authenticity, be mindful of overly curated or inauthentic accounts that can distort your sense of reality.

Name Your Savings Accounts

Instead of having one generic savings account, try naming them with specific goals: "Holiday Trip," "Emergency Fund," "Home Repairs," "New Laptop Fund." This helps you stay focused, motivated, organised and more connected to your goals.

Pause Before You Purchase

Before hitting "Buy Now", wait at least ten minutes after adding something to your online cart. That little buffer of time helps you avoid impulse buys and gives your brain space to decide if it's a true need, a meaningful want, or just a "meh, I saw it and clicked it" moment. Often, you'll find the urge passes, and your wallet will thank you.

Don't Fall Into the Sales Trap

When it comes to sales items, ask yourself: Would I still want this if it were full price? Do I have a clear use or need for it? Does it add real value to my life? If the answer is no, walk away proudly. You just saved your future self from more clutter and your wallet from an unnecessary hit.

My dad once said to me, "It's only a bargain if you actually need it. Otherwise, it's just clutter in disguise that came with a discount sticker."

Practice Gratitude for What You Already Have

When you regularly acknowledge what you already have, whether it's enough food, a safe place to sleep, or clean clothes, you are less likely to fill emotional voids with unnecessary spending. Gratitude quiets the craving for more possessions.

Decluttering Your Mind

Decluttering isn't just about clearing out closets, tidying your schedule, or getting on top of your finances; it's also about making space within yourself. Just like piles of stuff can weigh down your home, a cluttered mind filled with racing thoughts, endless tasks, and heavy emotions can leave you feeling scattered and drained. True simplicity isn't only about what's outside; it's also about cultivating calmness and clarity on the inside.

This idea is so important that I've devoted two whole chapters later in the book (check out the chapters on boundary setting and learning to let go) to helping you untangle mental and emotional clutter in deeper, practical ways. But here, in the context of simplifying your life, one of the most powerful first steps is to create a little sanctuary for yourself. A quiet space that's entirely yours, a place to pause, breathe, and let your mind settle.

In the next section, we'll look at how to design this personal retreat and make it a space that supports a calm state of mind, restores your energy, and reminds you that you always have somewhere to come back to when life feels full.

Your Sanctuary: A Tool For Mental Clarity

Below are some ideas to help you shape a space that supports inner calm, no matter your living circumstances. A place that feels like home to your soul.

Designate a Space that Feels Peaceful and Calming

Find a spot in your home where you naturally feel at ease. Let it become your personal retreat for when life feels overwhelming or stressful. It doesn't have to be fancy; as long as it feels like yours. A place where you can exhale. (Just watch out if you have a cat, mine has a habit of claiming every peaceful spot for himself. Apparently, he's into slow living too.)

Keep Your Space Clutter-free and Filled with Comfort

Let this be a no-clutter zone. Only include items that support calmness and comfort, maybe a soft throw blanket, a candle, a journal to write in, or a stack of uplifting books. The more this space feels like a visual and energetic exhale, the more likely you'll return to it regularly.

Incorporate Natural Elements

Add things that help ground you and soothe your senses like a plant or two (they boost mood and air quality), soft lighting (think warm-toned lamps or fairy lights), and calming colours like earth tones, soft blues or gentle greens. These small touches can make a big difference.

Keep It Ready to Use

Keep your sanctuary simple and always ready, even if that just means a clean corner with a cushion and your journal nearby. A low-effort setup increases the chances you'll actually use it.

Small is Fine, Get Creative

Not much space? No problem. Even a single chair near a window, a quiet section of your bookshelf, or a part of your balcony can become your retreat. Use what you have and make it feel intentional. The key is how it feels, not how big it is.

In Shared Living? Make your Bedroom Your Sanctuary

If you live in a share house or with a full family, your bedroom may be your only private space. Invest in soft bedding, add fairy lights, or curtains and keep it tidy and peaceful. Avoid making it a dumping ground for laundry or unfinished tasks; let it feel like your calm cocoon.

Use Scent to Set the Mood

Scent has a powerful connection to memory and emotion; it can instantly transport you to a calmer headspace. Use an essential oil diffuser, a roller blend, a candle, or even dried herbs or incense, whatever suits your vibe. Be aware of fire safety if using a live flame though!

Let Sound Support Your Serenity

What you hear in your space is as important as what you see. Soft instrumental music, gentle ambient playlists, or nature sounds like rainfall, ocean waves, or birdsong can instantly shift the mood and soothe your nervous system. They help drown out distractions and create a calm backdrop that keeps your mind from racing. Try keeping a peaceful playlist on low or use a white noise machine to create a more tranquil environment.

If your home tends to be noisy, consider investing in a good pair of noise-cancelling headphones; they can be a game-changer! And if the noise is your kids, try setting some gentle boundaries. Put a sign on the door or near you if it's a corner spot, make it into a game, maybe they earn a little treat if they give you some uninterrupted time. If there's another adult in the house, tag them in for support and if they distract the kids for you, they deserve a treat too.

Seasonal Touches

Swap out small elements in your space with the seasons: fresh flowers in spring, a soft knitted throw in winter, or a small bowl of pinecones or shells. These little changes keep your sanctuary feeling connected to the natural rhythms of the year.

Textures Matter

Add a variety of textures that feel comforting: soft cushions, a cozy blanket, a smooth stone, or even a small textured rug. Touch is surprisingly grounding and can make your sanctuary feel more inviting.

Natural Light and Views

If possible, choose a spot near natural light or a window. Even a glimpse of the outdoors, a tree, sky, or garden, can bring a sense of stillness and perspective.

Rotate Items

Keep things fresh by rotating a few elements, perhaps a new book, a different throw, or a new plant. Small changes make your sanctuary feel alive and prevent it from becoming stale.

Lastly Add a Personal Touch That Speaks to Your Soul

This is the secret ingredient that turns a space into your sanctuary. It could be a photo of a loved one, a favourite quote framed on the wall, a rock you picked up on a meaningful walk, or a little trinket that brings you peace. These small, sentimental items remind you of who you are and what matters most, helping you stay grounded, present, and emotionally nourished.

Practical Exercise: Create Your Mini-Sanctuary

Instead of just reading about it, let's have some fun and actually set up a calming space. Let's create your very own little retreat where you can pause, breathe, and reset.

1. **Pick your spot** – Wander around your home and notice where your body naturally feels "Ahhh." It

could be a cozy chair by a window, a quiet corner of your bedroom, a small space on the balcony, or even a section of your bookshelf. Don't overthink it, this is about feeling drawn to the space, not measuring square footage.

2. **Five minute sanctuary setup** – Give yourself just 5 minutes to make it feel inviting. Add one soft or cozy item, like a cushion, throw, or blanket; one natural element, such as a plant, shell, rock, or flower; and one personal touch, like a photo, candle, or small object that sparks joy. Don't worry about perfection; simplicity is key.

3. **Set the mood** – Create an atmosphere that calms and soothes you. Play a favourite relaxing playlist, light a candle or incense, or use a gentle scent that makes you feel peaceful. Even subtle touches, like soft lighting or a favourite mug filled with tea, can transform your space into a sanctuary.

4. **Now try it out** – Sit in your new sanctuary for a few minutes. Breathe deeply, let your body relax, and notice how different it feels to have a ready-made retreat waiting for you. Don't feel pressured to do anything, just be. Let yourself enjoy the small moment of peace.

5. **Build on the momentum** – Now that you've started, let your creativity flow! Explore what you already have around the house, maybe a treasured book, a cozy rug, a wind chime, or a basket for blankets. Add items that make you smile or feel comforted. Move things around, experiment with lighting or scents, and see what feels right. Make it playful and personal. The more you invest in it,

the more it becomes your special place to retreat and recharge.

Remember, your sanctuary doesn't have to be perfect or large. The magic is in the feeling it gives you. The goal is to create a space that feels like an invitation to slow down, breathe, and reconnect with yourself whenever you need it. This is your personal retreat, so have fun with it!

Heartbeat Of The Chapter

Simplifying your life is about more than just clearing physical clutter; it's about making space for the things that bring you joy, peace, and freedom. Each small step you take, whether letting go of unnecessary possessions, streamlining routines, or reducing commitments, lightens your load and makes life feel more manageable. By simplifying, you create room to breathe, think clearly, and be present with the people and activities that matter most to you. You make a conscious choice to choose quality over quantity.

Challenge This Week

This week, let's make life a little lighter. Pick one area to simplify. Just one! It could be:

- Physical: a drawer, your wardrobe, or your workspace, any space that tends to gather clutter and makes your day feel heavier than it needs to be.
- Financial: subscriptions you never use, messy bills, or spending habits that feel overwhelming. Clearing these can give you a real sense of control and calmness.
- Work or daily routine: long to-do lists, scattered priorities, or commitments that drain your energy without adding meaning. Simplifying here can give your days more flow and ease.

Now pick one small, manageable action. Maybe it's clearing your work desk, cleaning out that dreaded bottom kitchen drawer, or unsubscribing from unnecessary emails. Give yourself just half an hour to focus on it, more if you're feeling inspired, but even thirty minutes can create a noticeable shift.

After you've done it, take a moment to pause and reflect:

- How did your mood and energy feel afterwards?
- Did you notice a sense of lightness, clarity, or calmness that wasn't there before?
- Did you have a sense of achievement?
- Give yourself a high five for doing it!

STOP RUSHING *Start Living*

Every small declutter, every tiny simplification, is a gift to your time, your mind, and your sense of freedom.

Affirmation This Week

"I am ready to release what no longer serves me and make room for what brings me peace."

CHAPTER 7

Disconnect to Reconnect: The Path Back to You

> "When we unplug from the noise of the world, we remember the rhythm of our breath, the pulse of the earth, and the quiet truth of who we are."
> - Liz Anderson

I'm a dog person, I love my beautiful golden Labrador. He's a very relaxed and carefree doggy but he has a bad habit of eating anything and everything. If it's on the ground, he thinks it's for him, so down the hatch it goes. Unfortunately, this leads to an upset tummy every now and then and when he's feeling off, I've noticed something simple yet profound. The first thing he does is go outside and curl up on the grass in the sun. It's instinctual. He seems to know that touching the Earth and being in the sun helps him feel better.

In stark contrast, we humans seem to be the only animals on this beautiful, abundant planet who are largely disconnected from that natural source of well-being. We shut ourselves indoors, surrounded by artificial lighting, breathing in recycled air, and eat foods that might be convenient but are engineered to last months and are ultra-processed. When was the last time your bare feet touched the grass, or you stood outside to enjoy the feeling of the sunlight on your skin? When was the last time you looked at the wonderful world we live in and felt a sense of awe and connection to something greater than yourself?

We've built a world so full of digital noise and artificial comforts that we have become disconnected from what it is to be human and part of this world. We live in our artificial little bubbles: told what to think, what to buy, and what to eat by an algorithm that shows us what we want to see. A skewed version of a reality that's only one-sided. We've scrolled through sunsets instead of watching them. We've consumed moments instead of feeling them. And we've forgotten that life isn't meant to be managed by algorithms, it's meant to be felt, savoured, and truly lived.

We rarely allow ourselves the luxury of being still, without reaching for a screen or filling silences with more input. Reconnection begins not only in nature, but also in those small pauses where we step away from the noise and embrace silence, cut back on distractions and let ourselves breathe.

For me, nature has always been a place to reconnect, a way to reset and reenergize. Rainforests in particular, hold a special place in my heart. As a child, some of my fondest memories are of family holidays spent wandering down lush green trails, where every sense is awakened, the smell of damp earth, the sounds of the birds in the canopy and the gentle babbling of a creek in the distance. Whenever I immerse myself in nature, even if it's in my own backyard, I feel something shift. The constant buzz of the outside world fades. My mind settles. My breath deepens. Time stretches out, and I feel connected again to our Earth and my humanness, a connection so deep and profound that trying to describe it with words is almost impossible.

Why It's Important To Unplug

Disconnecting or unplugging looks different for each of us, and it's a deeply personal practice. At its heart, it's simply about giving yourself permission to step away for a while and do something that brings you peace, calmness, or joy. The benefits go far beyond just feeling calmer, such as:

Reducing Stress and Re-energising Our Body

Our nervous systems are constantly stimulated by the demands of modern life, leaving little room to rest and regulate. Regularly unplugging, even in small ways, helps lower cortisol levels, supports emotional balance, and creates space to breathe again. It also supports better sleep and brings us back into sync with our natural rhythms. But not all forms of unplugging are created equal.

Think about the last time you spent an entire day binge-watching a show. Sure, you may have shut out the world for a while, but did you actually feel refreshed afterwards, or did you feel flat and foggy? Now compare that sensation to the last time you went to the beach, took a walk in the woods, or even just sat in the sun for a while. Chances are, when you were in nature you felt clearer, lighter, and more alive.

The quality of our rest matters. That's not to say you should never enjoy a lazy TV day; we all need those sometimes, but don't make it your only way of switching off. Choose the kind of rest that truly revitalises you and fills you with joy and optimism, not one that only numbs you. Your body and your spirit will thank you.

Making Space for Deeper Thinking and Creativity

When we step away from the constant stream of input for a while, we give our minds the space to wander, wonder, and create. Our imagination needs silence to come to life. Daydreaming is actually a powerful gateway to creativity and problem-solving. It gives your imagination the freedom it needs to stretch and play. It also creates space for reflection and self-awareness (something we'll explore more deeply in the chapter on self-reflection). It helps us tune out the world long enough to actually hear our own inner voice and guidance. Think of how many brilliant ideas seem to appear while you're in the shower or on the toilet, those moments when the mind is quiet and free to roam.

Feeling More Grounded and Connected to the Earth

Nature has a way of reminding us that we are part of something far bigger. When we walk barefoot on the earth, watch clouds drift overhead, or listen to the sound of birds, we are brought back into alignment with the natural rhythms of life. This connection grounds us and offers a sense of peace that technology simply can't replicate.

It's an Essential Skill to Teach our Children

In a world that constantly pushes us to be busy and entertained, one of the greatest gifts we can offer the next generation is the ability to just be. Children need time to decompress, to sit with their own thoughts, and to experience moments of quiet without an agenda. They don't always need an activity or a screen to fill the silence.

More and more, teachers (and many of us parents) are noticing that children's ability to tap into their imaginations is becoming stunted. Creativity is giving way to consumption. It's reflected everywhere, from the struggle to come up with original ideas in the classroom to the endless remakes of old movies that flood our screens. By modelling the art of unplugging and embracing unstructured, screen-free time, we show them their inner world matters and that creativity thrives in silence.

How Do I Unplug And Reconnect?

Learning to disconnect and relax can be surprisingly challenging, especially if you're someone who's always on the go. For those used to being busy, slowing down can feel unfamiliar, even uncomfortable. You might find yourself watching the clock, waiting for your "break" to be over so you can get back to your to-do list. But the key is one I've already mentioned in earlier chapters: start small and ease into it.

You don't need to disappear into the wilderness for a week to feel the benefits of unplugging. Begin with a few minutes a day, five minutes of silence in the morning, a walk with your phone on silent, or simply sitting outside with a cup of tea, watching the world drift by. Build from there at your own pace. It's important that your reconnection time doesn't feel like another task to tick off.

Below are some simple ideas to help you unplug and reconnect in some common areas people struggle with:

Set Boundaries with Technology

Schedule Daily Unplugging Time

Block out thirty to sixty minutes a day to be tech-free. Walk, cook, meditate, or just be.

Turn Off Non-essential Notifications

Ditch the constant pings. Only keep alerts for important things (like calls or texts from loved ones).

Replace Screen Time with a Hobby

Pick up a forgotten passion or start a new one: drawing, puzzles, knitting, music, gardening, something that doesn't involve a screen.

Try a Digital Sabbath

Once a week, go screen-free for a whole day to reset your system and reconnect.

Use Grayscale Mode on your Phone

Making your screen less stimulating can reduce the urge to scroll endlessly.

Be Intentional with Tech Use

Before using your phone or device ask yourself, "Why am I doing this?" If there's no clear reason, or it's out of boredom, be intentional and choose another more nourishing activity.

Use an Alarm Clock

Use a real alarm clock instead of your phone to start your mornings without distractions. I guarantee you if you pick up your phone to turn off your alarm, the pull will be too great to resist checking your messages!

Read Books Instead of Scrolling

Our eyes and minds are constantly flooded with glowing screens, and that steady stream of light and stimulation can leave us feeling drained. Reaching for a good old-fashioned paper book offers a gentle alternative, a break for your eyes and a soothing reset for your brain. There's something calming about turning real pages, letting your imagination wander, and sinking into a story or idea without the constant pull of notifications.

Reconnecting at Work

Take Your Breaks

Use your breaks to reset your mind and body, step outside for fresh air if you can, even if it's just for five minutes.

Get Away from Your Desk

Stand up, stretch your legs, and move away from screens to release tension and refresh your focus regularly.

Take Mini-Breaks Every Hour

Pause for a minute each hour to breathe deeply, stretch, or adjust your posture. Tiny resets make a big difference.

Create Supportive Rituals

Add small, nourishing habits to your day, like mindful tea-making or walking at lunchtime.

Practice Presence in Conversations

Instead of multitasking while talking with colleagues, give them your full attention. Close your laptop, silence notifications, and really listen. People can feel the difference when they are truly heard, it builds stronger, more authentic connections.

Step Into Natural Light

Whenever possible, swap fluorescent lighting for sunlight. Even spending a few minutes by a window or stepping outdoors will reset your energy and remind you that there's a world beyond your screen.

Bring Nature In

Add a plant, a small flower, or even a natural object (like a stone, seashell, or wood piece) to your desk. These little reminders of the natural world can be surprisingly grounding in an otherwise artificial environment.

Use Transitions Intentionally

Like we touched on in the chapter on mindfulness, the moments between tasks or meetings present an opportunity to pause, breathe, or stretch. Treat transitions as mini-reset points to reconnect with yourself before diving into what's next.

Redefine Productivity

Take a step back and reconnect with the reasons why you are working. Productivity isn't just about how many emails you send or tasks you check off; it's about the bigger picture. Think about the people you're helping, the skills you're developing, and the values you're living out through your work. And don't forget the personal benefits too: the holidays you can take, the day trips you can enjoy, and the special experiences your income makes possible. When you recognise the deeper purpose behind what you do, the small tasks become more meaningful.

Reconnect with Nature

Take a Daily Walk

Whether it's a walk in the park, by the beach, or through the woods, being in nature clears the mind and resets your energy. Set your intention to reconnect with nature, and the walk will feel that much more meaningful and enjoyable!

Practice Grounding

Walk barefoot on grass, sand, or soil to reconnect with the earth's energy and feel more centred. A quick little exercise is to close your eyes, take a slow breath, and press your feet firmly into the ground. Imagine roots growing from the soles of your feet deep into the earth, anchoring you. With each breath, feel yourself becoming steadier, calmer, and more present. Let all your stress and tension leave via your feet into the Earth. You can also do this sitting down, just watch out for ants, they like to bite your bum!

Start a Garden

Even if it's a few plants on a balcony, caring for something living fosters patience, joy and reconnects you with the rhythms of nature.

Sit in Silence Outdoors

Find a quiet spot outside, close your eyes, and listen to the sounds of nature, birds, rustling leaves, or the wind.

Join a Hiking/Bushwalking Group

Walking with others motivates you to continue the practice and is a great way to increase your social circle with like-minded people.

Go on a Mystery Drive

Pick a direction and drive; explore what's out there. You'll be surprised at the little treasures you come across.

Watch a Sunrise or Sunset

This experience is very relaxing and grounding, no equipment necessary, just your attention.

Eat Outside

Whether it's your morning coffee or your evening meal, eating outside can add presence to your meal and elevate it.

Volunteer for a Local Conservation or Garden Project

It's a great way to get outdoors, give back and meet people with similar interests.

Reconnecting with ourselves and others

Sit in Silence

Take a few minutes each day simply to sit in stillness. It may feel uncomfortable at first, but silence is where you can meet yourself again. (There's a practical exercise in the next section to help you get comfortable with silence.)

Use Prayer or Positive Affirmations

Whether through prayer, gratitude, or affirmations, quiet the noisy internal chatter by speaking kind and uplifting words to reconnect you with your inner strength and something greater.

Put Your Phone Away When Socialising

When you're with someone, give them your full attention. It's one of the greatest gifts you can offer. If you're on a time limit, set a quiet alarm on your phone, or even better, let the person know upfront what time you'll need to leave. That way, you can both relax, be present, and make the most of your time together.

Practice Compassion and Kindness

Being of service, big or small, reconnects us with the heart of who we are and reminds us of our shared humanity.

Listen to Music or Look at Art that Stirs Your Soul

Find the songs, sounds, or visuals that give you goosebumps and make you feel something deeper.

Move Your Body with Awareness

Gentle movement like stretching, yoga, or dancing reconnects you with your body and releases built-up tension. It's not about exercise for performance but about tuning in and listening to your body.

Practice Deep Listening

When talking with others, focus less on what you'll say next and more on truly hearing them. Listening without interruption or judgment deepens relationships and reminds us that connection is a two-way street.

Spend Time in Nature with Others

Invite a friend or loved one for a walk outdoors. Being in nature together makes it easier to drop the distractions and simply enjoy each other's company.

Practical Exercise: Getting Comfortable With Silence

Getting comfortable with silence is both important and quite challenging for many of us. I struggled with it at first, but now I treasure those quiet moments, moments where I can simply be, enjoy peace, and let my mind and imagination roam freely.

In today's world, we're so used to constant background noise that silence can feel almost intolerable at first. That's why it's worth building up your "silence tolerance" gradually. For some, this will be easy, so feel free to skip ahead if that's you. For others, it may feel uncomfortable at first, but practising in small increments makes it increasingly easier and feel more natural.

Here's how to start:

- **Pick one quiet moment this week** – aim for at least five minutes to begin.

- **Choose a simple activity** – it could be a walk with your phone on silent, sitting in the garden noticing the sounds around you, eating a meal without screens or background noise or even just pottering around the house in silence.
- **Notice your experience** – pay attention to how your body feels, what thoughts arise, and any small sparks of clarity or creativity.
- **Reflect briefly** – afterwards, jot down anything you observed: Did you feel calmer or more present? Did your mind wander in interesting ways? Did any ideas, insights, or inspirations appear? Were you uncomfortable? Did any anxious thoughts or feelings arise?
- **If difficult thoughts or feelings came up, that's okay.** Many people shy away from silence because it can bring uncomfortable thoughts and feelings to the surface. But avoiding silence for that reason only makes life feel smaller and noisier, as we keep trying to drown those thoughts out.

With time and practice, you will be able to meet these thoughts and feelings in a new way, one that softens their grip and reduces their impact. Tools like mindfulness, gratitude, and other practices we'll explore later in this book, such as letting go and self-reflection, will be beneficial too.

When challenging thoughts do arise, gently guide yourself back to a calm balanced state of mind by using the strategies we covered earlier: focusing on your breath, grounding through your senses, or repeating a soothing affirmation.

Liz Anderson

Heartbeat Of The Chapter

When we unplug from distractions, we create room to reconnect with what's important to us, our natural rhythms, our creativity, and our sense of wonder. Life stops feeling like a race to be run and instead it becomes a series of moments to be felt, experienced, and savoured.

Letting our mind rest and wander, free from the loudness and speed of modern life, opens the door to rediscovering joy, imagination, and awe in the world around us. These moments of silence and reconnection return us to ourselves, remind us of our shared humanity, and gently guide us back into mindfulness and gratitude.

Challenge This Week

Your challenge this week is to spend some time in nature with the intention of reconnecting to yourself and the world around you. Find a nice spot, which could be a park, your backyard, a community garden, or even a nearby street with trees. If going outside is difficult, find a spot by a window where you can see plants, the sky, or natural light.

Spend at least ten minutes in this space (do more if you wish), focusing on your surroundings. If you're outside:

- Touch the earth: place your hands or bare feet on the ground, grass, or tree. Feel the texture beneath your fingers and your feet. If you're inside, look out your window at the clouds, the trees, or any plants near you and really look, taking in the patterns, colours and movements of nature.

- Listen: close your eyes for a moment and listen to the sounds around you, birds, wind, distant traffic, or the rustling of leaves.
- Breathe deeply: take slow, deep breaths. Inhale the air around you, and exhale any tension and stress.

Try to do this twice during the week, ideally on different days. Each time, give yourself a few quiet moments to simply be present in nature and, afterwards, take a moment to reflect.

- Did you feel calmer and more clear-headed?
- Did you find it enjoyable?
- Did you get any sparks of inspiration or creativity?

Affirmation This Week

"I know that when I disconnect from the noise of the world, I reconnect with my purpose, my joy, and my inner wisdom."

CHAPTER 8

The Power Of Boundaries: Creating Space For What Matters

"Daring to set boundaries is about having the courage to love ourselves, even when we risk disappointing others."

- Brené Brown

When I first started working for myself, I thought, finally, I'll have the work/life balance I was craving. No boss, no office hours, no commute, my dreams were finally becoming a reality. I was being more mindful, practising regular gratitude and looking after myself, so surely life would finally slow down and become more manageable.

But work continued to seep into every area of my life. I was still answering emails outside of my work hours, writing notes and reports on weekends and taking calls on my days off. The line between work and my personal life remained blurred. I resented the fact that my work was taking up more real estate in my head than I liked. Instead of feeling free, I was always on and always tired; it was not the work/life balance I was hoping to achieve. It took a while for the penny to drop, but I finally realised that I had neglected to do any work around my boundaries. That's when it began to make sense to me.

I had done all the "easy" internal work, the parts that mostly depended on me, but I'd avoided the harder steps, the ones that required me to set boundaries with others. That's where it became complicated, because stepping into that space meant facing emotions like disappointment, guilt, and the fear of letting people down.

But I knew I had to do this part if I wanted to see real change. So I took a deep breath, put my big girl pants on and started to draw some hard lines, like setting strict work hours, making certain days off-limits for anything work-related, resisting the urge to check my work messages "just quickly" and saying no to unnecessary commitments. Once I did that, I began to reclaim my time and my energy. That's when the other things I had been adding into my life, like mindfulness, gratitude and self-care, started to make a difference in a bigger way. They weren't just quick fixes to get me through the day anymore; they were really shaping the way I felt and how I moved through my life.

Setting boundaries is powerful. They give us breathing room, protect our energy, and allow us to invest it where it matters most. In many ways, this ties directly back to what we explored in the chapter on simplifying and decluttering. Setting boundaries is like weeding a garden: you remove what drains your energy so there's space for growth, beauty, and the things that lift you up.

Now, it's important to note here, not everyone will respect your boundaries or respond the way you'd like, and that's okay. We'll cover how to handle the likely pushbacks later in this chapter. But first, let's look at the other important benefits of boundaries and how they can enhance your life in more ways than you think. Boundaries also:

Enhance Your Emotional Resilience

Healthy boundaries support this by giving you stability and breathing room. Instead of constantly reacting in the heat of the moment, boundaries create space to pause, process, and respond with clarity, even when life is overwhelming.

Help Us Develop Self-care and Self-respect

Many people associate boundary-setting with being cold or detached, but in reality, it's an act of deep self-respect and self-care. When we set boundaries, we affirm to ourselves and others that our time, energy, and emotional well-being are as valuable as anyone else's.

Enhance Decision-Making

With boundaries in place, you're less likely to make impulsive, people-pleasing or guilt-induced choices. Instead, you will make decisions that align more with your values and goals.

Improve Relationships

Setting clear boundaries fosters healthier relationship dynamics, whether in friendships, family, work or romantic partnerships. By defining your boundaries and communicating them openly, you reduce misunderstandings, clarify expectations, and minimise the risk of resentment building up over time. Boundaries create mutual respect, ensuring that all parties feel heard and valued.

Of course, while the idea of setting boundaries sounds simple in theory, in practice, it can be challenging and uncomfortable, especially if you're accustomed to putting everyone else's needs before your own.

The Struggles Of A People-Pleaser

Hands up all the people pleasers? You know who you are. The ones who can't hear the words boundary setting without breaking into a cold sweat. Just the thought conjures up visions of awkward confrontations, disappointed glances, guilt-laced silences, or the crushing weight of someone else's disapproval.

Maybe you've been there, standing on the edge of a no, heart pounding, already rehearsing your explanation while simultaneously imagining all the ways it might go wrong. You picture the sighs, the looks, the tension. You feel the pressure rising, not just from others, but from inside you too. Because somewhere along the way, you learned (or were trained) that being good meant being available, agreeable, and self-sacrificing.

But here's the thing. You can be kind and still have boundaries. You can show up for others without losing yourself in the process. I know setting boundaries won't be easy; things worth doing rarely are. Expect that the guilt will still creep in. The fear of letting someone down might still whisper in your ear. But with practice, it gets easier. You're allowed to choose yourself, without explanation, without guilt, and without apology.

So How Do You Know If You're a People-Pleaser?

We all fall into some of these habits every now and then, it's totally normal. But if the behaviours we're about to cover are showing up for you more often than not, it could be a sign that you're sliding into people-pleaser territory. If that's the case for you, then learning how to set healthy boundaries isn't only a good idea, it will be a game-changer!

Some of the common traits of people-pleasers are:

- Avoiding conflict at all costs, even if it means sacrificing personal needs or opinions.
- Over-apologising, even when it's unnecessary.

- Difficulty saying no and struggling to turn down requests.
- Overcommitting to avoid letting others down.
- Sacrificing your personal needs and putting the needs of others over your own well-being.
- Suppressing or hiding emotions to prevent upsetting others.
- Feeling overwhelmed and stressed from trying to meet other people's expectations.
- Struggling with setting and maintaining your personal boundaries.

The People-Pleaser's Challenge: You Don't Have to Fix Everything

Another common challenge for people-pleasers is a compulsion to fix everything. But guess what? You weren't put on this Earth to solve everyone's problems. It may feel like that at times, but it's important to work out whether others have put this expectation on you or whether you you've put it on yourself. It's a difficult assessment to make, especially if it involves the people you love and care about. However, constantly rescuing or overextending yourself only leads to exhaustion, resentment and unhealthy dependency.

More importantly, we rob others of the opportunity for growth and self-discovery if we're always there to take on their load and/or to save them.

Here's an example to illustrate what I mean. Let's say a friend constantly comes to you to solve their problems, whether it's financial help, emotional support, or handling tasks they could manage themselves. Instead of immediately stepping in, try gently redirecting them by offering encouragement or suggesting resources they can explore on their own. This response not only protects your energy but also empowers them to take responsibility which may lead to real personal growth. It's not about abandoning people, it's about trusting that they are capable, even if they don't believe it yet.

Now, don't get me wrong, it's perfectly okay to help and support others. As a society, it's important that we're community-minded, act with kindness, and have empathy for those around us. However, people-pleasing takes this to a whole new level, often at the cost of your own physical and mental well-being. Every time you say yes to something to please another person or go along passively to keep the peace, you are saying no to something that matters to you. You deserve to save your energy and time for the people and things that bring you joy and fulfilment.

Please be aware that I'm not sharing this information on people-pleasing to make you feel bad or add another layer of pressure. As I said before, we all fall into some of these patterns from time to time. The purpose is simply to help you notice if people-pleasing has become your default mode. Awareness is the first step towards change. If you recognise yourself in several of these traits, it doesn't mean something is wrong with you, it means that it will be useful for you to examine and evaluate the boundaries you currently have in place and how you can enhance and strengthen them. The good news is, with practice, support, and a few shifts in how you interact with others, you can absolutely reclaim your energy, your confidence, and your sense of self.

General Tips For Boundary Setting

Start As Early As Possible

The earlier you set a boundary, the better. While it's absolutely possible to introduce a new boundary later on, it will be more challenging to shift expectations that have already been established. Setting boundaries from the beginning, whether it's in a new relationship, a job, a friendship, or with your kids, creates clarity and consistency right from the start.

For example, if you're starting a new job and want to protect your evenings, you might say:

"I'm always happy to give 100% during the workday, but I'm unavailable after I finish at 5pm."

That kind of clarity early on makes it easier for others to respect your time and for you to uphold it.

If you didn't set the boundary early, don't let that stop you. Even though it may require additional time, patience and persistence to establish it, it will happen.

Be aware that it is also perfectly ok to change and adjust your boundaries as you grow and your needs change.

Be Honest

When setting a boundary, honesty goes a long way. You don't owe anyone an explanation for your boundaries but if someone pushes or asks for one, being truthful is usually the best approach. Honesty helps others understand where you're coming from and reduces confusion or guilt.

Let's say a friend invites you to the movies, but you've had a long week and really need some downtime. **Here's how that conversation might go, along with how to express your boundary clearly:**

Friend: "Hey! Want to catch a movie tonight? It's been forever since we've hung out!"

You: "I'd love to see you soon, but I've had a really long week and I'm feeling drained. I need a quiet night to recharge."

Friend: "Oh come on, it'll be fun! You can relax at the theatre!"

You: "I get that, and I really appreciate the invite. But let's pick another day when I can be fully present."

This kind of honesty sets a clear boundary without guilt or over-explaining. It also gives you space to care for yourself while you are showing up in your relationships with integrity.

Communicate Clearly

When setting boundaries, be clear and concise with your language. Don't leave anything open to interpretation, or be vague, or passive-aggressive in your responses. Clear communication avoids misunderstandings and sets respectful expectations from the start. The more direct you are, the easier it is for others to understand and honour your needs.

For example, let's say a coworker consistently text messages you after hours, expecting quick replies. **Instead of hinting that it's inconvenient, be upfront:**

Coworker: "Hey, just wanted to check if you can take a quick look at this tonight?"

You: "Hi I've committed to not checking work messages after 6 p.m. so I can fully unplug in the evenings. I'll happily take a look first thing tomorrow morning though."

Coworker: "Got it, just thought it might be quick!"

You: "I totally understand, and I appreciate you reaching out. I'm just making sure I stick to this boundary so I can be more effective during work hours. Talk to you tomorrow."

This kind of clear communication respects your time and teaches others how and when to engage with you without leaving space for misunderstandings.

You Don't Always Have to Tell Others about Your Boundaries

Sometimes, the most powerful boundaries are the ones you quietly hold within yourself. You don't always need to announce them, especially when the person you're setting the boundary around is difficult or prone to confrontation.

Let's be honest, we all have people in our lives who, when we see their name pop up on our phone, we let out a weary sigh. In these cases, internal boundaries are your best friend.

You might not say out loud, "I'm only going to talk to them for ten minutes," but you can decide that for yourself and stick to it. You might choose to let their words wash over you without taking them personally. You might opt not to engage in certain topics or mentally remind yourself, I don't have to explain or defend myself.

Here's an example of what I mean. Let's say you have an aunt who always brings up your parenting style or comments on your appearance. Rather than confronting her directly every time, which might lead to more stress than it's worth, you can set an internal boundary. Maybe you only stay at the family gathering for a set amount of time, or mentally prepare by reminding yourself not to take her comments personally because she's a cow to everyone. You might plan to politely excuse yourself when certain topics come up or shift the conversation to something neutral.

Remember, boundaries are also about choosing how you engage with people or situations and what you allow to affect you.

Boundaries Aren't Just for Other People

We often think of boundaries as something we set for others but we can also set them for ourselves. They keep us grounded in what we know is good for our body, mind, and soul. This might look like having set work hours, not checking your phone before 8 a.m. or committing to a daily walk. Think of the boundaries you set for yourself as gentle guardrails that keep you aligned with your values and the kind of life you want to live.

Practical Ideas for Setting Boundaries

Now that we've looked at tips for setting boundaries and why they matter, especially if you tend to put others' needs before your own, let's turn to some practical ideas for using them in everyday life.

Below is a menu of possibilities. Think of them as gentle prompts to spark your own thinking. You definitely don't need to try them all, just notice which ones feel relevant or supportive for you right now, and leave the rest.

Digital Boundaries

- Set screen time limits on your phone for social media, news, or entertainment apps.
- Establish "no-phone" zones in your home (e.g., bedroom, dining table, bathroom).
- Create a digital curfew, like turning off devices or putting your phone on "Do Not Disturb" after a certain hour.
- Turn off non-essential notifications so you're not constantly being pulled away by pings and pop-ups.
- Set boundaries with others about when and how you respond to messages and phone calls (for

example, "I don't respond to texts or calls after 8 p.m. unless it's an emergency.").
- Keep your phone out of reach during focused activities like reading, journaling, or spending time with loved ones.

Time Boundaries

- Decline last-minute plans if they interfere with your rest, routine, or priorities.
- Set meeting limits (for example, "I have thirty minutes available for this call").
- Politely say no to invitations or favours that you don't have the time, energy or don't want to do.
- Create "Do Not Disturb" times at work or home if people frequently interrupt your focus time.
- Limit social time if you're feeling overextended and prioritise quality over quantity.
- Communicate ahead of time when you need uninterrupted personal time (e.g., "I'm offline this weekend to recharge").
- Block out time for rest or hobbies, and treat it as non-negotiable.
- Use a calendar or planner to schedule personal time just like you would meetings or errands.
- Avoid overcommitting by pausing before saying yes and checking your availability, or say you will get back to them, just make sure you do.
- Give yourself permission to do nothing; downtime is productive too.

Work Boundaries

- Set clear work hours and stick to them.
- Protect your break times and step away from your desk, eat lunch without working, and give your brain a chance to recharge.
- Create a dedicated workspace (especially if working from home) so you can mentally switch off when the day ends.
- Practice saying no or setting limits when your workload is already full (e.g., "I can take this on next week, but not right now").
- If you manage others, delegate when possible and model healthy boundaries so your team members will follow your example.
- Decide how much overtime (if any) you're willing to do and make it the exception, not the rule.
- Don't automatically take on tasks outside your job description unless you choose to.
- It's okay to excuse yourself from gossip, office politics, or conversations that drain your energy.
- If you're working remotely, make it clear when you're online and when you're offline, so colleagues don't assume round-the-clock access.
- Decline unnecessary meetings or ask for an agenda before agreeing, so you protect your time.
- Notice which types of tasks or people deplete you and, where possible, structure your day to do them in short, intentional bursts instead of letting them take over.

Emotional Boundaries

Up to this point, we've looked at boundaries that are a little easier to define, things like time, technology, and work. But when it comes to emotions, the lines are blurry and often complicated. These are the boundaries that touch our closest relationships where love, loyalty, and guilt get tangled together. It is why emotional boundaries are often the hardest for us to set and the easiest to let slip.

But they are also the most important because they protect our inner peace and allow us to show up with genuine care rather than resentment or exhaustion. Let's look at some common ways to recognise, create, and maintain healthy emotional boundaries.

Notice Your Emotional Limits

Start paying attention to how you feel around certain people. Do you often leave interactions feeling drained, anxious, or overwhelmed? These emotional signals are clues that a boundary might be needed. You don't have to be harsh, but you can gently distance yourself from relationships that are consistently draining. It's okay to limit your time with people who manipulate, guilt-trip, or constantly put their emotional burdens on you without reciprocating.

What Can I Do?

Write down or simply take note of the moments when you feel emotionally overextended. Identify the people, situations, or patterns that trigger these feelings. **Once you've recognised them, ask yourself:**

- Do I need to limit my contact with this person or situation?
- Do I need to set a clear boundary?

If so you can do this in two ways:
- Directly, by having an honest conversation about what you need.
- Indirectly, by deciding on the boundary for yourself and adjusting how you interact with them (for example, spending less time with them, changing the topic when needed, or creating more emotional distance).

Either way, the goal is to protect your emotional well-being and create a space that is safer and more balanced for you.

Don't Take on Other People's Emotions

Of course, you want the best for the people in your life. You want to be there for them, to listen, to help, but that doesn't mean you are required to carry or absorb their emotional load. You can care deeply about someone and still protect your own emotional energy.

I call this detached compassion. It's the ability to be supportive and present without absorbing someone else's stress, sadness, or anger as your own. In this situation, your spiritual or personal philosophy really comes in handy. Quietly reminding yourself, "This is their journey, not mine," will ease the guilt that sometimes shows up when you set emotional boundaries. (Please don't say that statement to someone who's in the middle of a crisis. They probably won't appreciate the spiritual wisdom in the moment. But keeping it in the back of your mind will assist you to stay grounded rather than being pulled into the drama.)

What Can I Do?

Remind yourself: "This is their emotion, not mine. I can support them without carrying it." Or "This is their journey, not mine."

You can also try visualising a protective energy barrier around yourself. One simple and powerful technique is imagining you're inside a white or golden bubble of light. This bubble is strong but gentle; it allows love, compassion, and care to flow out from you, but it deflects anything negative or heavy from coming in. Imagine stress, anger, or drama bouncing off the surface and dissolving, without touching your energy field. You're still present, but you're protected.

This visualisation can be especially helpful before or during emotionally intense conversations, or when you know you're going to be around someone who tends to drain you. Think of it as energetic self-care, like an emotional coat of armour.

Set Boundaries Around Venting and Oversharing

Saying no or stepping back when someone's constant venting or oversharing starts to feel draining doesn't make you a bad friend, partner, or family member. It simply means you're honouring your own limits and protecting your emotional well-being. It's wonderful that people feel comfortable opening up to you, but that doesn't mean you have to be their personal therapist every time you get together.

What Can I Do?

Try setting limits in advance, or if you find yourself in the middle of a draining conversation, use one of these gentle but firm boundary statements as an example:

- "I'm sorry, I've had a long day, and I don't think I'm in the best place to talk about this right now. Can we catch up about this [person, situation, problem] again soon?"
- "Hi, I've only got ten minutes to talk because I have an appointment to go to."
- "That sounds really hard for you and I'm sorry you're going through this [situation, problem, difficulty]but can we talk about something a little lighter?"

If it's a text, remind yourself that you don't have to respond right away. Give yourself permission to pause and reply later, when you're prepared and have the emotional space.

Protecting your energy isn't selfish; it's what allows you to show up as a supportive friend, partner, or family member in a way that feels healthy and sustainable.

Know You're Not Responsible for How Others Feel

One of the most freeing truths you can embrace is: you are not responsible for how other people behave, react or feel, especially when you're being kind, honest, and respectful.

The truth is, other people's emotional reactions are shaped by their experiences, expectations, wounds, and current state, not just by your words or actions alone. You can be doing everything right, and someone might still get upset, which doesn't mean you've said or done anything wrong.

What Can I Do?

Gently remind yourself: "Their reaction isn't my responsibility if I'm being kind and respectful." This is a powerful mindset shift that will enable you to hold your ground without falling into guilt, feeling manipulated or slipping into people-pleasing patterns.

When someone is upset by your boundary, pause and take a breath. Ask yourself:

- Was I clear and kind in my communication?
- Did I act in alignment with my values and needs?
- Am I honouring both myself and the other person by being honest?

If the answer is yes, you can release the responsibility for how they choose to feel or respond. Just because someone doesn't like your boundary doesn't mean you shouldn't have it.

Recognise When Something Feels Off

When something doesn't sit right with you, whether it's how someone's speaking to you, how often they're relying on you, or just the general vibe of an interaction, it's important to acknowledge it and decide if action is needed.

What Can I Do?

When you notice that something feels off, pause and ask yourself:

- What exactly is bothering me here?
- Do I need to say something, or do I set up an internal boundary around this issue?
- If I do say something, how can I express this clearly and without blame?

If you decide to speak up, use "I" statements to take ownership of your feelings and make the conversation less defensive.

For example: "I've been feeling really drained lately. I care about you and want to support you, but I also need a bit of space to take care of myself right now. Can we talk about this another time, or shift the conversation for now, please?"

Or

"I feel uncomfortable when jokes are made about me in front of others. I know it might be meant playfully, but it doesn't sit well with me."

It might feel uncomfortable in the moment, but chances are it will lead to better boundaries, a healthier connection, and at the very least, more peace and happiness for you. All worthy goals.

"No" Isn't A Dirty Word

Don't be afraid to say no, it's a form of emotional self-care and goes hand in hand with setting boundaries, especially emotional ones. It doesn't mean you're being rude, cold, or selfish; it does mean you're being honest about your limits and what you do and don't want to do.

We all have a limited amount of time, energy, and mental space. You're allowed to not do something for no other reason than because you don't want to do it. It's that simple. No apology. No explanation required. People who care about you will understand, and the ones who don't probably need a boundary anyway.

How To Say No

Keep It Simple

When a short, respectful "no" isn't enough, don't be tempted to make a big speech or over-explain. Just get comfortable with some gentle but clear ways to say no.

Try:

- "I'd love to help, but this week's already kind of packed."
- "I appreciate you asking, but I've got too much on my plate."

Be Honest, but Kind

You can be clear without being harsh. Most people will respect you more for being upfront.

Try:

- "I'm really trying to keep my schedule lighter right now."
- "I've been saying yes too often and need to slow down a bit."

Offer an Alternative (If You Want To)

You don't owe anyone a workaround but if you genuinely want to help, suggest something else that works better for you.

Try:
- "I can't meet this week, but how about next Tuesday?"
- "I don't have time to take this on, but maybe check with..........?"

Delay Your Response

If you feel put on the spot, it's okay to pause and come back to it. Delaying your response gives you time to decide what you actually want.

Try:
- "Let me check my schedule and get back to you."
- "Can I think about it and let you know?"

Trust That 'No' is a Complete Sentence

You don't have to manage other people's reactions. If someone pushes back, stay firm. You're not responsible for their feelings; but you are responsible for your own well-being.

You Are Allowed to Change Your Mind

If you've said yes to something and then have that sinking feeling of *Why did I agree to that?*, remember, you're allowed to change your mind. It's okay to reassess, especially when saying yes no longer feels right. It's far better to be honest than to push through with resentment or burnout. Changing your mind doesn't make you flaky, it means you're listening to yourself and respecting your limits.

Try:
- "I'm sorry, but after thinking about it more, I won't be able to do this after all. I hope you understand."

- "I realised I overcommitted, and I need to step back from this. I really appreciate your understanding."

When people push back

Let me start by saying that nine times out of ten people to whom you've said no will simply move on, it's no big deal. We're often the ones who make it bigger in our own minds because we don't want to let others down or feel guilty. But in reality, a respectful no is rarely as dramatic or damaging as we imagine. Often, people appreciate the honesty and even respect you more for being up front about it.

But sometimes, people may question you, try to guilt you, or keep pushing in the hope you'll change your mind and give in. This can feel uncomfortable, especially if you're new to setting boundaries and saying no. The key is to stay calm, repeat your message if needed, and avoid getting pulled into long justifications.

Here are some ways you might respond in real-life situations when people push back:

If someone says, "You've changed" or "You never used to have a problem with this".

Try:
- "I'm learning to take better care of myself, and this is part of that process."
- "You're right. I've been rethinking what I need to stay well, and I'm trying something different."
- "That's true, and I've realised the old way wasn't working for me."

If someone tries to guilt-trip you try:

- "I understand this might be disappointing, but I need to honour what feels right for me."
- "I hear that this isn't what you were expecting, but I'm making choices based on what I need right now."
- "Saying no is hard for me too, but I need to do this for me."

If someone keeps pushing after you've said no try:

- "I've already shared my decision."
- "I know this isn't what you were hoping for, but I'm standing by my decision."
- "Please respect this boundary. I need you to hear me."

If you feel the need to soften without backing down try:

- "This boundary isn't about rejecting you, it's about protecting my energy."
- "I care about our relationship, and having boundaries helps me stay present and connected when we're together."
- "I need to say no to this request to look after myself and my well-being."

Setting emotional boundaries is one of the most challenging and courageous things we do, precisely because it involves our deepest feelings and often the people we care about most. It asks us to stand in our truth, even when it's confronting and uncomfortable.

Each time you hold your boundary or say no, you're proving to yourself that you can survive discomfort and come out stronger.

Practical Exercise: Creating Boundaries That Stick

In this exercise, we will explore how to identify where you might need boundaries, how to set them with intention, and how to uphold them with confidence.

Step 1: Identify Areas Where You Need Boundaries

Take a moment to reflect on your life and ask yourself the following:

- Where do I currently feel stretched too thin?
- What activities, commitments, or relationships drain my energy and well-being?
- Where in my life do I need to say no more often?

Step 2: Define Your Boundaries

Now, let's turn those reflections into clear, actionable boundaries. For ease, let's use the format below for writing your boundaries.

I will [your boundary] because [your reason], and I will communicate it by [what action you will take]

Here's a few examples of boundary statements:

I will not check work emails outside of my designated work hours because I need a better work-life balance. I will communicate my availability to colleagues by setting an auto-reply.

I will limit my social media use to thirty minutes a day because I want to be more present in my life. I will organise this boundary by setting app limits on my phone.

Okay, your turn, write down a few boundaries in your life using the above format.

Step 3: That was the easy part—Now comes the challenge

Identifying your boundaries is a great first step, but the real work begins with putting them into action. Take some time to think about how you'll express your new boundaries in a way that's kind and firm. Practise saying them out loud, either on your own or with someone you trust. It can also be helpful to have a few go-to responses ready in case someone doesn't respond well to your boundary.

- How will you communicate your new boundaries to those around you?
- What will you do if someone pushes back on a boundary?

This kind of preparation will build your confidence and ease some of the anxiety that can come with these conversations. Remember, you're not being harsh, you're being honest about what you need in order to take care of yourself. So well done on looking after you!

Remember, boundaries aren't about building walls; they're about creating healthy spaces where you and your relationships can thrive. Don't forget to check out this week's challenge at the end of the chapter to put your new boundaries into action.

Heartbeat Of The Chapter

By now, you have a clearer sense of where boundaries might be useful in your life, whether with others, at work, at home, or even within yourself. You've explored practical ways to define those boundaries, along with simple tools and phrases to communicate them with confidence, kindness, and clarity.

The key reminder here is that boundaries are not selfish. They are acts of self-respect and self-care. Each time you say no to what drains you, you're saying yes to what matters most. Boundaries protect your time, energy, and well-being so you can live with more balance, clarity, and intention.

Every boundary you set, no matter how small, is a step toward a healthier, more grounded way of living. Keep going, one boundary at a time. The more you honour your needs without guilt or apology, the more natural it will be and the more space you create for the life you truly want to live.

Challenge This Week

Now that you've done the groundwork, it's time to take action. Choose one of the boundaries you developed in the exercise above, just one, and begin putting it into place this week. It can be a direct boundary (something you communicate to others) or an indirect boundary (something you set for yourself).

Start with a boundary that is meaningful but manageable, something small enough to stick with, but important enough to make a difference.

At the end of the week, take a moment to reflect:

- How did it feel to put this boundary into action?
- In what ways did this boundary make your life more manageable or aligned?

When the time feels right, introduce another one. Little by little, these small shifts are reshaping your daily life. Each new boundary is a step towards living with more intention, self-respect, and inner peace.

Affirmation This Week

"I am learning to protect my energy and wellbeing by setting up and communicating healthy boundaries."

CHAPTER 9

Learning to Let Go

"The beautiful journey of today can only begin when we learn to let go of yesterday."

— Steve Maraboli

"Just let it go."

"Get over it."

"Just move on."

We've all heard these phrases at some point, sometimes from well-meaning friends and family, and other times from people who simply don't want to deal with our emotions. On the surface, letting go sounds simple, straightforward, logical even.

But let's be honest, you're a thoughtful, intelligent person. If it were just a matter of flipping a mental switch and moving on, you would have done it already and be off living your best life, unburdened by the past.

The truth is, letting go is one of the hardest things for us to do. It's something that comes up again and again in my work with clients. They come to me with the same question: "How do I let go and move on when I've tried but can't stop thinking about it?"

Take my client Sophie (not her real name) for example, she came to therapy feeling stuck after the sudden breakdown of a close friendship. Her friend had pulled away without explanation, leaving her replaying conversations over and over in her head and longing for answers and closure.

She was caught in a painful loop of self-doubt and what-ifs. She said, "I know I should let it go, but I can't. I need to understand why."

Through our work, Sophie realised she was holding on to the need for answers that might never come. Together, we focused on self-compassion, acknowledging her hurt, validating the importance of the friendship, and recognising that the ending was out of her control. She practised small acts of release, like journaling what she wished she could say and creating a goodbye ritual.

Letting go didn't mean forgetting; it meant making peace with uncertainty and choosing not to carry a story that no longer served her. As Sophie said later, "The closure I was looking for had to come from me. I had to let it go."

This shows that letting go is a process, not about erasing the past, but about finding peace and acceptance within yourself when answers never come or things are out of your control.

Why Is Letting Go So Hard?

We hold onto things for all kinds of reasons, because they hurt us, because they changed us, because they shook something deep within us. Sometimes we're not aware of how much we're still carrying and it leaks out in ways we don't expect such as through anxiety, overreactions, relationship struggles, or that constant mental replay of an incident or relationship we wish had played out differently.

What we hold on to can range from deep psychological wounds (trauma, abuse, abandonment) to smaller everyday moments like a hurtful comment, a mistake that keeps haunting us, an unresolved argument, or a sense of being misunderstood.

But no matter the scale, the emotional weight can be very real. And the decision we face, again and again, is how can I let this go so I can move on in peace?

Letting go isn't about pretending things don't matter. It's not about minimising your pain. It's about learning how to process it, so it doesn't control you. Holding on to negative emotions like anger, resentment, disappointment or sadness doesn't make us strong; it makes us vulnerable and keeps us stuck. Whereas, letting go is empowering, positive and allows us to move forward again in our lives.

Why Is It Important?

Letting go is one of the most powerful, freeing acts of self-love we can offer ourselves. It's how we create space for healing, clarity, peace, and growth. When we hold on to painful memories and emotions, we often don't realise how much energy it takes to keep carrying those weights around. Over time, that burden quietly drains our joy, clouds our judgment, and keep us anchored to the past rather than living fully in the present. Here's why letting go matters so deeply to our emotional health:

- As we touched on in our chapters on decluttering and setting boundaries, letting go clears the clutter in your mind and heart, making space for more positive, nourishing emotions like peace, joy, and hope.

- Constantly dwelling on the past and holding onto past hurts keeps our stress response switched on. It's like being stuck in a time loop that prevents us from getting on with our life. Letting go means allowing ourselves to move through the pain instead of living in it endlessly. When we loosen our grip on old wounds, we give ourselves permission to heal, learn, and grow from the experience, rather than letting it define who we are.

- When we're stuck in unresolved hurt or anger, it affects how we relate to others, especially those closest to us.

- Letting go helps us return to now, the only place we can truly experience peace, make empowered choices, and build the kind of life we want.

OK, So How Do I Let Go?

Letting go doesn't mean denying the impact of what happened or sweeping it under the rug. It's not about pretending it didn't hurt or acting like it didn't matter. In fact, it's quite the opposite.

The process of letting go begins with acknowledgment and facing the very thing that's causing us emotional pain. That's why it's so hard. It asks us to stop running from the feelings we'd rather not deal with. Instead, we do need to feel them, sit with them, and begin to understand them.

Ask yourself:

- How did this make me feel?
- Why does it still affect me this way?
- What does it bring up about how I see myself or how I see others?
- Was I in control of what happened? Or was I doing the best I could at the time?

This kind of deep reflection can be incredibly confronting, especially when it involves someone important to us, or when it forces us to look at parts of ourselves we're not proud of. That's why so many people choose to push things aside. They say, "I'll deal with that later." But later never comes.

Take, for example, someone who's still haunted by a comment a parent made years ago, maybe something like "You'll never be good enough." It's easy to dismiss it as careless words but the emotional echo of that moment could be shaping how they see themselves today. Until they face it, that comment continues to live rent-free in their mind, influencing parts of their life they are probably not even aware of.

Or consider someone who made a mistake, maybe they hurt someone they care about or failed at something important. The shame can be so uncomfortable that, instead of processing it, they bury it and avoid it. But unprocessed shame doesn't disappear. It lingers and shows up in ways we don't always expect, like self-doubt, self-sabotage, anxiety or depression.

Unfortunately, life isn't all joy and light. To move through it fully, we have to feel the full spectrum, the messy, uncomfortable emotions too. It's only by feeling them that we can release them. Letting go means facing the pain, understanding it, and then choosing not to carry it with us every day.

Think of your emotional life like a filing cabinet. You can only fit so much in there. If you never clear out the old files, the grief, the grudges, the guilt, it becomes harder and harder to make space for joy, connection, and new experiences. Letting go is like cleaning that cabinet regularly. You don't need to keep every painful memory front and centre. Some things, once acknowledged and understood, can be archived or even discarded.

You don't have to forget. You don't have to pretend it didn't matter. But you can decide it doesn't get to rule your life anymore. There is power in that decision. There's healing. There's freedom.

Acceptance

A vital part of letting go is acceptance. It's one thing to recognise what we've been holding onto, but the real question is, what do we do with it now? The next step is accepting that some things are out of our control, whether it's something that has already happened or something we cannot change.

Just like in Sophie's case, she longed for answers about why her friend had pulled away. She only started to heal when she accepted that those answers would never come. She couldn't change what had happened, but she could change how she let it affect her life from that moment on.

This is the heart of acceptance. It doesn't erase the hurt, but it transforms our relationship with it. When we acknowledge, yes, this happened and I can't change it, but I can choose how I respond now, we loosen the grip of the past and create space for healing, peace, and new beginnings.

Where Does Forgiveness Fit In?

Whenever I bring up the topic of forgiveness with people, I receive a lot of resistance and a whole list of reasons why that is NEVER going to happen. But in most cases, once I explain what forgiveness actually means and how freeing it can be for people, they warm to the idea and agree to give it a go. Then, inevitably, somewhere along their therapy journey, it always comes up as one of the most empowering things they ever did.

The concept of forgiveness is deeply woven into the process of letting go. In many ways, it's the emotional and spiritual bridge between pain and peace. Without forgiveness of others and of ourselves, letting go often remains incomplete. It's like trying to walk forward while still dragging a heavy anchor behind you.

When we hold on to resentment, anger, or hurt from what someone else has done, we often believe that holding on gives us a sense of justice or control. "If I let this go, it's like saying it was okay." But in reality, it means you are choosing not to let it impact you anymore.

Forgiveness is an act of reclaiming your own peace. It doesn't require reconciliation. You don't have to let someone back into your life. You don't even have to tell them you've forgiven them. It's an internal process, a choice to stop allowing their actions to take up space in your mind, heart, and identity.

Self-Forgiveness

Then there's the even harder part of forgiveness, which is forgiving yourself.

This is where many people get stuck. We replay our mistakes, our regrets, the things we said or didn't say, the chances we didn't take, or the people we hurt (intentionally or not). We wear shame and guilt like armour, believing that if we punish ourselves enough, we'll somehow earn redemption.

But self-punishment never leads to healing, only more pain.

Forgiving yourself doesn't mean ignoring accountability. It means:
- Acknowledging what happened.
- Taking responsibility (when appropriate).
- Learning from it.
- And then giving yourself the grace to grow beyond it.

Forgiveness of self is the compassionate voice that says, "I am human. I've made mistakes. I've learned. I am still worthy of love and peace."

It's an act of deep self-compassion, one that lets you move ahead lighter, wiser and more whole.

Forgiveness is often the gateway to letting go. Letting go is the act. Forgiveness is the tool that helps make that act possible.

Letting Go Of The Things You Can't Change

We have control over our own thoughts, actions, and attitudes. We don't have control over other people's choices, behaviours, or feelings. And while understanding that distinction is important, really accepting it is much more difficult.

One of my favourite, though admittedly unpopular, sayings is, "If you can't change something, the only real option you have is to change your attitude about it." I use this saying with my kids when they complain about having to go to school. I'll remind them that school isn't optional right now and that fighting that reality only makes them more miserable. They can choose to change their attitude, find something positive in the experience, or at least make peace with it and accept it. (Of course, this usually earns me a severe eye roll, but the message still lands!)

Learning to shift your mindset when you can't change your circumstances or how someone acts, is not only freeing, it's empowering.

A great example of this is when we bravely decide to speak our truth. What I've learnt over the years, both in my own life and in my work with clients, is that we often don't get the reaction we hoped for. Especially when we're confronting someone about how their words or actions have impacted us. We might crave acknowledgment, understanding, maybe even an apology. But most of the time that's not what we get, and it's completely out of our control.

For example, we have a family friend. They're well-travelled, intelligent and also deeply frustrating. Generous and kind in many ways but exhausting to be around. They're always right, their way is the only way, and everyone else's thoughts are mildly amusing at best.

The kind of person you only see once a year, and when you do catch up, you remember exactly why you only see them once a year!

One year, after a particularly irritating interaction, I hit my limit. We had just moved into a new house and were craving a quiet, low-key Christmas, but they were demanding, not asking, to come and stay for a few weeks. I was overwhelmed, stressed, and not in the mood for what felt like a toddler on a sugar high, sprinting through our lives, demanding constant attention.

So, I wrote them an email. I took my time, weeks actually, putting it together. I poured my feelings out carefully. I had my husband, my brother, and my mother read it to make sure it was firm but kind, honest but not cruel. I wanted them to get it. To understand why people struggled with their behaviour. And, maybe, just maybe, make some changes.

When I received a reply, I could hardly believe what I was reading.

They had completely ignored the heart of my message. They had cherry-picked a few neutral lines and responded to those, completely bypassing the actual point of the letter.

But here's the surprising part. I wasn't upset. In fact, I felt strangely at peace. That experience taught me three life-changing lessons:

1. The act of expression is more important than the response.

Writing that email was my way of processing, releasing, and feeling heard, even if the other person never listened. It was not about their reaction. It was about unburdening myself.

2. It's unfair to expect someone to change if they aren't capable or willing to see themselves clearly.

They didn't behave that way just with us. It wasn't personal; it was simply who they were. That realisation freed me from feeling targeted or hurt. They weren't out to annoy me specifically. They were just being themself.

3. The only thing I can control is myself, my reaction, my boundaries and my energy.

This part was the most empowering for me. I began to manage my expectations and my interactions with them. I learned to steer conversations away from triggering topics, to share less and to simply accept them as they were. And with that acceptance came peace.

Now, when I interact with them, it's so much easier. They haven't changed, but I have. And that's made all the difference.

Many times when you're processing a past hurt or disappointment, like in my example, it's not necessary for healing to receive the other person's acknowledgment, apology, or even understanding. You don't even have to let them know about it. Because most of the time, they simply aren't capable of giving you what you're hoping for.

So when you're faced with a situation beyond your control, whether it's someone else's behaviour, work politics, or even world events, start by asking yourself, "How can I change my attitude towards this person or situation?"

Focus on what you can control, like your attitude, your boundaries, and your actions. Letting go isn't about ignoring problems or pretending everything's fine; it's about freeing yourself from the stress of trying to fix the unfixable. By practising this approach, you reclaim your power, your peace of mind and navigate challenges more effectively. You may not be able to change the situation, but you can always change how you deal with it.

Techniques For Letting Go

Over the years, I've worked with people navigating everything from deep, life-altering trauma to everyday irritations that quietly wear them down. In the process, I've learned that the tools we use to let go are less about erasing the pain and more about transforming our relationship with it.

Whether you're holding grief that refuses to soften, carrying the sting of betrayal, struggling with shame, anger, or replaying the one moment that makes your stomach turn, these tools are here to support you. While not quick fixes, these practices enable you to acknowledge what you're feeling, to process it with care, and begin to create space for healing. Let's look at some of the common letting go techniques.

Writing to Let Go

I've always found writing to be one of the most powerful tools for people to release what they've been holding onto. It creates a dedicated space to feel deeply, to process honestly, and to pour emotions onto the page that may have been locked away for years. It's a kind of emotional exhale: a raw, unfiltered mental and spiritual release.

There's something almost alchemical that happens when we physically engage the body, especially the hands, in emotional processing. Writing can act like a signal to the brain and heart: I'm ready to let this go now. It brings what's been swirling around in your mind into the light, where it can be seen, understood, and released.

Here's how to get started:

Set the Scene

Find a quiet, uninterrupted space where you feel emotionally safe (like your personal sanctuary). Let others know you need some time alone. Light a candle if that feels grounding. Grab a pen and paper (yes, pen and paper, it isn't about typing neat little sentences on a screen). Keep a box of tissues nearby. Let this be a sacred moment between you and your inner world.

Begin the Release

Start writing. Don't overthink it. Dump everything out onto the page, no filters, no rules. Swear, cry, scribble, rant, even stab the page if you need to. It is about getting the emotions out of your body and onto the paper.

If you feel stuck or unsure where to begin, use these prompts as a guide:

- What is the issue or situation I'm struggling to let go of?
- Why did this affect me so deeply?
- How does it make me feel about myself, about others, about the world?
- What story am I telling myself about this situation?

- Has it impacted other areas of my life, my relationships, self-esteem, or choices?
- Was there anything I could or couldn't control?
- How do I wish things had gone differently?
- Did I play a part in this? If so, what can I learn?
- How has this shaped who I am?
- What has this taught me about myself?

Let the answers come naturally. You don't need to resolve it all in one sitting. This is about honesty, not perfection. You might write a little or pages and pages. There is no right or wrong, let it come out in whatever form and flow it takes.

What Next? Burn It. Rip It. Keep It.

Once you've written it all out, you get to choose what happens next. Some people find it incredibly cathartic to burn or tear up the paper as a symbolic act of letting go. Others prefer to keep their pages as a record of emotional progress. Do what feels most empowering and healing to you.

Guided Meditations and Visualisations for Release

Visualisations and guided meditations can be a powerful way to help release stuck emotions. Most of our memories aren't stored in words; they're sensory. We remember in images, feelings, smells, and bodily sensations. That's why visualisation is especially helpful when it's difficult to put our experience into words.

You can visualise all kinds of scenarios to support emotional release, but here are a few simple and effective ones I regularly use with clients and myself.

Cutting Ties

This visualisation is helpful when you're ready to energetically disconnect from a situation, person, or experience that no longer serves you.

- Find a comfortable position and gently close your eyes.
- Take three deep, grounding breaths. With each exhale, allow stress and tension to leave your body. With each inhale, feel yourself becoming calmer and more relaxed.
- Bring the person, situation, or emotion to mind. See it clearly in your mind's eye. Notice any feelings or sensations it brings up in your body, and observe without judgment.
- Now imagine a rope or cord connecting you to it. This cord can be any colour, material, or thickness; it's uniquely yours. Visualise where it's attached to you and to the other person or situation.
- Now, imagine cutting the cord. Choose whatever tool you like: a sword, giant scissors, a bolt of lightning, anything that feels powerful to you. It might take some effort. You might need help from your guides, angels, God, or your higher self. Ask for support if you need it.
- When you've cut the cord, watch it fly back, taking all the negativity and emotional weight with it. Let

it return to wherever it came from, leaving you lighter and freer.

- Take another three deep breaths and open your eyes.

You can return to this practice any time you feel reattached or weighed down. There's no limit to how often you can cut energetic cords.

Blasting it to the Sun

This is a more playful but effective visualisation for when you need to release something fast.

- Take a deep breath and bring to mind the thing you want to release.
- Now, imagine a rocket ship in front of you. Begin placing all those feelings, thoughts, or burdens into the rocket. Maybe they look like little creatures, clouds, or blobs, use whatever your imagination desires.
- Close the rocket ship door, step back and count down: 5... 4... 3... 2... 1...Blastoff! And launch the rocket into the sky. Watch it soar higher and higher until it reaches the sun where it explodes into golden light, dissolving completely along with all things you put inside.
- Take another deep breath and notice the lightness and space left behind.

You can do this any time you need to, even multiple times a day if needed.

Sun Breathing

This is a gentle, grounding practice that uses the healing warmth of the sun to help release emotions and restore inner serenity.

- Find a sunny spot, by a window, in your backyard, or anywhere you feel safe and warm.
- Close your eyes and feel the sun on your skin. Let its warmth wrap around you like a soft, comforting blanket.
- Visualise the emotions or energy you want to release. See them as coloured clouds inside your body, wherever you feel them most.
- With each breath in, imagine drawing in golden sunlight. This light fills your body, slowly pushing those clouds of emotion downward.
- With every breath, the light pushes the clouds lower, through your chest, your belly, your legs, until they exit through your feet and into the earth. The Earth receives them with love and transforms that energy into something positive.
- Feel your whole body filled with golden light, peaceful, warm, and strong. Let yourself rest in that feeling.
- Take a few deep breaths, and when you feel ready, gently open your eyes.

These visualisations exercises are simple, but powerful. Use the ones you feel drawn to or make up your own. The only limit is your imagination.

Speaking it Out Loud

Sometimes the most healing thing you can do is say it out loud.

Whether you're talking to a therapist, a trusted friend, or even just yourself in the car, giving voice to what you're feeling can be incredibly liberating. When we speak our thoughts out loud, what was once tangled and heavy in our minds begins to take shape. Personally, when I hear myself say something out loud, I can finally feel it, question it and release it. When we speak, we activate different neural pathways than when we're silently thinking. Speaking brings a level of conscious awareness that thinking alone doesn't always reach. It helps us name our emotions, organise our thoughts, and hear ourselves with more compassion.

If you're not ready or able to talk to someone else, voice journaling (literally recording yourself talking) can be a great alternative. You can just press record and let it all out, like a stream of consciousness. There's no pressure to make it perfect or polished. You can delete it after or save it to reflect on later. The important part is that you're expressing it, not bottling it up.

I've even suggested my clients talk to their pets. They don't talk back and they always listen. You can even talk to your house plants!

Whether you're venting in the shower or spilling your heart to your fern, speaking things out loud can be a powerful step in the process of letting go.

Breathwork and Somatic Release Exercises

Breathwork and somatic exercises are powerful tools for releasing built-up tension and emotional stress in the body. They help us reconnect with ourselves on a deeper level by inviting awareness back into the physical body, something we often lose touch with when we're caught in cycles of overthinking, worry or emotional overwhelm. These practices gently shift us out of our heads and into the present moment, allowing the body to process and release what is being held onto.

Below are some simple breathwork and somatic exercises designed to support the process of letting go. As you move through them, bring to mind whatever you want to release, and let each breath or movement serve as a pathway for stuck energy to move.

Remember, as we explored in the chapter on intention, the power lies in where you place your focus. If your intention is to use these practices to let go, that is the outcome they will guide you toward.

Box Breathing
- Inhale for four counts.
- Hold for four counts.
- Exhale for four counts.
- Hold the exhale for four counts.
- Repeat for four rounds.

Progressive Muscle Relaxation
- Lie down in a comfortable position.

- Tense a muscle group (like your fists, calves, or shoulders) for a few seconds and then release the tension quickly.
- As you release the muscle, focus on the sensation of relaxation and the contrast between tension and ease.
- Move through the body, focusing on one muscle group at a time, releasing tension and bringing awareness to any physical sensations.

Exhale Release Exercise
- Sit comfortably with your feet flat on the floor and hands resting on your lap.
- Take a slow, deep breath in through your nose, imagining your chest and belly expanding like a balloon.
- As you exhale through your mouth, sigh the breath out with a soft "haaah" sound, as if you're fogging up a window.
- With each exhale, picture yourself releasing a little bit of tension, heaviness, or stuck energy.
- Repeat for five to seven breaths, then sit quietly for a moment and notice how your body feels.

Creative Expression (painting, dancing, music)

Creative activities like painting, poetry, and other forms of self-expression can be incredibly powerful tools for releasing emotions and letting go of pent-up feelings. They provide a safe space to explore, process, and release emotions that might otherwise remain unspoken or bottled up, especially when putting things into words feels difficult. For example, you might paint a stormy sea to release feelings of overwhelm, write a poem to capture sadness, or dance out frustration until your body feels lighter. The key is to let your intention guide the creative act, so that the process itself becomes a trigger for release.

How Often Do I Have To Let It Go?

Now, I wish I could tell you that doing just one letting go exercise will wrap everything up in a neat little bow, that you'd do it once, feel instantly better, and never have to revisit that topic again. But unfortunately, our brains don't work that way (which frankly, is rude). The truth is, letting go is rarely a one-time event. It's often a process, a layered, sometimes frustrating, sometimes liberating journey that may take a few tries, a mix of different techniques, and a whole lot of patience.

You might try journaling, visualisation, talking it out, meditating or some combination of all of these techniques. Some days it might feel like you've made huge progress, and other days might bring up fresh waves of emotion you thought you'd already dealt with. That's completely normal. Healing and letting go are not linear; it's more like a spiral, bringing us deeper each time we revisit the experience, giving us new perspectives, and slowly loosening the grip it has on us.

That's not to say the memory will disappear. In fact, it won't. But over time and with practice, the emotional intensity it stirs up will fade. Instead of feeling like an open wound, it becomes more like a scar, still there, still part of your story, but no longer as sensitive or painful to touch.

Eventually, you will find you can look back on it with a little more neutrality, or even wisdom. You'll know you've started to shift when you can think about the situation or person calmly without having a lot of emotion arise. You will be able to view it with greater dispassion, as something that happened, not as something that defines you.

Practical Exercise: Let's Write A Letter

We've explored many ways to let go, now it's time to try one in action. For this exercise, it's best to choose something relatively light and not emotionally charged. If you've experienced trauma or deeply painful challenges, this might not be the right time and place to revisit them on your own without strong support around you. In those cases, working with a therapist or mental health professional can provide the safe guidance you need. But for everyday worries, frustrations, or smaller emotional burdens, this exercise can be a helpful way to begin learning to let go.

Step 1:

Find a quiet space where you won't be interrupted. Grab a pen and paper, and a box of tissues just in case!

Step 2:

Think of something you're ready to let go of, a feeling, a situation, a memory, or even a limiting belief. Take a few deep breaths and bring it to mind.

Step 3:

Write a letter to this thing you're releasing. You might start with:

"Dear [anger/shame/person/situation/etc.], here's what I've been carrying..."

Let the words flow. Be honest, raw, and unfiltered. Express how it made you feel, how it's impacted you, and why you are choosing to let it go. Use some of the questions below as a guide if you are not sure what to write:

- What is the issue or situation I'm struggling to let go of?
- Why did this affect me so deeply?
- How does it make me feel about myself, about others, about the world?
- Has this issue or situation impacted other areas of my life, my relationships, self-esteem, or choices?
- Was there anything I could or couldn't control?
- How do I wish things had gone differently?
- Why do I want to let this go?
- What did I learn from this experience?

Step 4:

End your letter with a statement of release, such as:

"I release you now. I no longer need to carry this burden. I choose peace, healing, and freedom."

Step 5 (Optional):

If it feels right, safely destroy the letter, burn it, tear it up, or bury it. Let the act symbolise your release.

After you've done this exercise, take a few quiet moments to notice how you feel. Do you feel lighter, clearer, or perhaps a little more at peace? Or maybe it brought up emotions you weren't expecting like grief, anger, sadness, even relief. All of it is valid. Let yourself sit with whatever has surfaced, without judgment. Sometimes, what we write reveals layers we didn't even know were there.

Heartbeat Of The Chapter

Hopefully, this chapter has helped you see just how vital the practice of letting go is for your emotional well-being and personal growth. Letting go isn't a single act, it's an ongoing journey of releasing the old stories, patterns, and emotions that weigh you down and hold you back from the life you truly want to live.

It's important to remember that letting go doesn't happen all at once, and that's perfectly okay. Healing takes time. But with every conscious choice to release what no longer serves you, you create more space for clarity, peace, joy, and expansion. Letting go is not about forgetting or pretending things didn't happen. It's about freeing yourself to move ahead in your life with more lightness and grace.

As you continue to practise what you've learned, know that each small step counts. Over time, these moments of release become powerful turning points. You will feel more grounded in the present, more open to what's ahead, and more in tune with who you really are. This is the path to emotional freedom and it's one worth walking.

Challenge This Week

If you completed the "Let's Write a Letter" exercise, try revisiting it later in the week and repeat the process, focusing on the same topic. Notice how your experience shifts the second time around. Did anything new arise? Are the emotions still present, or have they softened, changed, or even deepened? Was it easier or harder to let go this time? Letting go often unfolds in layers, and sometimes a second attempt offers even greater clarity, healing, or emotional release than the first. It's all part of the process.

Affirmation This Week

"I give myself permission to let go of the thoughts, stories, and emotions I've been carrying that no longer serve me."

CHAPTER 10

The Power of Self-Reflection

> "Knowing yourself is the beginning of all wisdom."
>
> - Aristotle

I drive a lot for work. I'm a mobile psychologist, but for many years, I was tied to a small office, four walls, no window, fluorescent lighting, and back-to-back appointments, sometimes seeing up to eight people a day with only a few minutes in between. While I truly loved the work and the people I helped, the environment wore me down. The constant churn, the artificial light, and the lack of fresh air slowly drained me. I felt as if I was suffocating.

I craved sunlight, space, and freedom. I wanted to breathe again. So, I made a bold decision and ditched the office and took my work on the road. I began meeting clients in their homes, at local cafés, and even by the beautiful lake in my suburb. Not only did it reconnect me with the world outside, sunshine, fresh air, and the rhythm of nature, but it also allowed me to reshape my schedule. Without office rent to pay, I could reduce my caseload and build more breathing room into my day by having a half hour between each client.

That space between clients, those thirty-minute drives, quickly became sacred. They became my me time. Time to reflect, recalibrate, and reconnect with myself. I'd talk to myself as I drove, asking questions like, "How am I doing? How am I feeling?" Sometimes I'd give myself a pep talk when I needed a boost, or offer a quiet word of praise for showing up for myself that day.

At first, it felt a little strange talking to myself out loud in the car. I was self-conscious, wondering what people might think. But then I noticed how many other drivers were chatting away on hands-free calls, and I realised no one could tell the difference. So I let go of the awkwardness and leaned into it. These little daily check-ins became a surprisingly grounding ritual, one of the cornerstones of my slow living practice, little moments of self-connection I wouldn't trade for anything.

My moments of self-reflection became more than just a habit; they became a way of tuning in to the inner compass that keeps me connected to my values and intentions. These pauses helped me stay true to the path I wanted to walk. In many ways, they were small signposts along the journey, simple moments that reminded me where I was heading, why it mattered and nudged me back on track when I took a detour.

And this is why self-reflection is so important. It gives us the space to pause, take stock, and gently adjust before we find ourselves overwhelmed or off track.

What Is Self-Reflection?

Self-reflection is pressing pause for a few intentional moments, whether once a week or even daily, to check in with yourself and take the pulse of your inner world. It doesn't need to be complicated. It might look like a five-minute chat with yourself in the car, a quiet moment on the back patio after work, a heartfelt conversation with someone you trust, or simply sitting in stillness and noticing what's going on inside your head.

These little pauses are powerful. They give you the chance to catch small issues before they snowball, to adjust your course gently in real time, and help you stay aligned with your deeper goals and intentions. They're also an opportunity to recognise what's going well, to celebrate the ways you're showing up for yourself and, at the very least acknowledge the progress you've made.

Self-reflection pulls together all the threads of slow living like mindfulness, gratitude, self-care, simplifying, setting boundaries, and letting go, into one clear practice, helping you to see what's working and where some adjustments might still be needed.

And perhaps the most important benefit of regular self-reflection is that it strengthens your relationship with yourself, helping you meet your own thoughts and feelings with honesty, compassion, and a deeper sense of understanding.

Building A Better Relationship With You

The most important relationship you'll ever have in life is the one you have with yourself. It's the foundation for everything else. Learning how to become your biggest supporter, rather than your harshest critic, is one of the most powerful skills you can develop.

All of us have two inner voices. One is positive, supportive, encouraging, and compassionate. The other – my friend Tania jokingly calls it the "Bitch in the Attic" – is the critical, negative voice that can be harsh, unhelpful, and downright unpleasant at times.

The goal isn't to silence that self-critical voice completely (because it's part of being human), but rather to shift the balance. By regularly checking in with ourselves in a compassionate, understanding way, like we would with a dear friend, we start to strengthen the helpful voice. Over time, that kind, supportive inner dialogue becomes louder, and the critical one loses its power and is silenced faster.

By giving yourself understanding and care, you strengthen and deepen your relationship with you, creating a foundation of self-respect, self-compassion and emotional resilience.

Liz Anderson

Being Emotionally Responsible

Doing regular check-ins with yourself isn't only to notice how you're doing and give yourself high fives. It's also about taking ownership of your emotions and the part you play in your own life. In my private practice, I often meet people who are kind, thoughtful, and genuinely good-hearted, yet they struggle to see how they might be contributing to the very challenges they face. It's common to hear things like, "Everyone around me is the problem," "No matter what I do, nothing ever works out," or "If they would just change, I'd finally be happy."

The truth is, and it's not easy to admit, but sometimes it's our own actions or inactions that determine the outcomes we get. We all make mistakes, fall into old patterns, or react in ways we regret later. It doesn't mean we've failed; it simply means we're human. What matters most is how we respond in those moments. The empowered choice is to recognise our role, accept it with compassion and self-forgiveness, and use it as an opportunity to learn and grow.

This is where regular self-reflection becomes so powerful. By slowing down enough to ask yourself questions like, "What part did I play in this situation or outcome?" and "What can I do differently next time?" you begin to cultivate emotional maturity, resilience and a growth mindset.

Sometimes these self-reflections also invite an even deeper philosophical perspective of "What is this situation trying to teach me right now? Is it patience?

The courage to stand up for myself? Or perhaps the wisdom to finally let something go?"

Self-Reflection: How To Do It

When I help clients establish a self-reflection practice, I often suggest starting with a simple daily routine. You don't need to overcomplicate it; just a few thoughtfully chosen questions are enough. Think of it like having a conversation with a close friend. What would you genuinely want to ask them about their day, their mood, or how they've been handling life's challenges?

Once you've settled on your go-to questions, write them down and keep them somewhere visible, like your bedside table, tucked into a journal, or in a little corner of your personal sanctuary. These gentle reminders make it easier to build a habit at the start, and over time, you'll find the questions come naturally without needing a prompt.

It's important to remember that self-reflection isn't about judging or criticising yourself. It's about checking in honestly, noticing how you're feeling emotionally, mentally, and physically, and giving yourself the space to learn, grow, and adjust along the way. This practice helps you stay grounded, connected to yourself, and aware of the progress you're making.

End each reflection on a positive note. Even on difficult days, look for a small win or gratitude, a moment of kindness you offered or received, or simply acknowledge the effort it took to keep going.

Celebrate the small, steady steps and offer yourself encouragement. Over time, these moments of pause will become a source of insight, resilience and self-compassion, helping you navigate life with greater clarity and intention.

Practical Exercise: My Check-In Questions

Let's take this opportunity to create a list of go-to questions for your self-reflection practice. They don't need to be fancy or profound, just a few simple prompts that help you explore how your day has been. If it helps, imagine a friend sitting across from you and consider what you might ask them about their day.

Here are some examples to get you started:

- How am I feeling right now, emotionally and physically?
- What went well today?
- What challenged me today, and what can I learn from it?
- Are there any adjustments I need to make in my life at the moment?
- What is one small thing I can do for myself right now?

Now, take a few minutes to write down three to five questions of your own. Once you've written your questions, keep them somewhere accessible, type them into your phone, jot them in your journal, or write them on a card or piece of paper (bonus points if it looks beautiful!).

Now you're ready to get started!

Heartbeat Of The Chapter

Self-reflection is a powerful way to stay grounded, resilient, and aligned with your intentions and goals. By pausing to notice what's working, what's hard, and how you're really feeling, you give yourself the gift of clarity and compassion. Reflection isn't about judgment; it's about curiosity, kindness and taking ownership of your growth. Even a few quiet minutes in the car or with a journal can create meaningful shifts over time. When you make self-reflection a habit, you catch problems earlier, celebrate wins more often, and keep moving closer to the life you truly want, one honest check-in at a time.

Challenge This Week

Now that you've created your self-reflection questions, take some time this week to put them into practice and notice how it feels. Carve out a few minutes each day, even five minutes is enough, to check in with yourself using your questions.

End each check-in by offering yourself a kind word or affirmation, for example:

- I'm doing the best I can, and that's enough.
- I handled that well today! Good on me!
- I am allowed to make mistakes, to learn from them and grow.

Let this week be the start of a self-reflection practice that's flexible, supportive, and uniquely yours, a practice that nurtures awareness, growth, and a deeper connection to yourself.

Affirmation This Week

"I honour my journey by pausing, reflecting, and learning. With each reflection, I connect more deeply to my true self and embrace the wisdom within."

CHAPTER 11

How to Make Lasting Change

"Be the change that you wish to see in the world."

- Mahatma Gandhi

Change is hard. Really hard! If it were easy, everyone would do it. I'd be out of a job, the diet industry would vanish, and the world would probably be a much better place. The truth is, change takes effort, it takes time, and, most frustratingly, it often feels like two steps forward and one step back.

We sabotage ourselves without even realising it. We get impatient. We expect quick results and when things don't change fast enough, we feel discouraged or convince ourselves it's not worth the effort or worse, we decide there's something wrong with us.

I spent years, decades really, trying to manage my weight. I was always on the lookout for the next quick fix, the latest fad diet, trendy life hack, bestselling book, some miracle gadget or convenient solution that promised effortless weight loss. If it claimed I could drop pounds without really changing much, I was in.

I'd buy into it, get excited, maybe stick with it for a few days, sometimes a week if I was really motivated. But when the magic didn't happen fast enough (or at all), I'd toss it aside and start hunting for the next "secret" solution. I kept hoping that this time, it would be different.

What I was really searching for was a way to lose weight without actually having to do the work, without having to change my habits. I didn't want to eat less, move more, or give up the comfort foods I loved. I wanted results without discomfort. Change without sacrifice. I wanted to keep doing what I was doing, but somehow get a different outcome.

At one point, I even had gastric bypass surgery. And while it was a successful procedure, it helped me eat less and gave me a helpful tool, I still had to do the same things I'd been avoiding all along, eat nutritious food, move my body and stay consistent. The surgery didn't let me skip the work; it just made it more manageable.

Eventually, after forty years of chasing shortcuts, I finally took on the message. There's no magic button. No hack, no product, no perfect program. It's the boring, unglamorous stuff that actually works. Eating well. Moving more. Being consistent. It takes effort, it takes time, and yes, it can be inconvenient and annoying. But it's real. And it works. When I came to that realisation, I went through what felt like a grief period. I was really bummed out by it. It was like mourning the loss of the fantasy that something would swoop in and make it all easier for me.

But once I accepted the fact that change is meant to be gradual, not instant, it became easier to stop searching for that magical solution and start doing the things that steadily moved me toward my goals.

But Why Is Change So Hard?

Well, in the wise words of Shrek (yes, the ogre), we're like onions. We have layers. So much of what drives our behaviour lies beneath the surface: habits, beliefs, emotional patterns, even our nervous system. And peeling back those layers? It's uncomfortable, it's vulnerable and it takes time.

I've seen it over and over again. A client comes in, motivated and ready for change. They throw themselves into it, start a new routine, quit a bad habit, shift their mindset. And for a while, it works. They feel amazing, like they've finally cracked the code. But then life happens. Things get busy. Something unexpected throws them off course. And suddenly, they find themselves right back in the old patterns they were trying so hard to break.

When they come back to me, they're often frustrated, dejected and confused. "Why am I doing this again? I know better."

And that's when I share with them that when people try to change everything all at once, they get burnt out. They try to do too much too fast. At first, it feels great, like a honeymoon phase, but just like honeymoons, that feeling doesn't last. When stress hits or life gets messy, we default to what's familiar, even if it's not helpful, because it's what we know, and our brains are wired to seek comfort in what's familiar, even if it's what we're trying to change.

But the people who create lasting change do it differently. They go slowly. They pick one or two small things to focus on, and they stick with those until they become second nature. Then they build on that. Step by step, layer by layer.

It's not glamorous. It's not fast. But it works.

Like the tortoise in Aesop's fable, it's the slow and steady ones who win the race. Not because they're more disciplined or more determined, but because they understand that real change isn't about speed, it's about building something sustainable, one small choice, one small step at a time.

The Stages of Change: Why Change Happens In Phases

One helpful framework for understanding how people make lasting change is the Stages of Change model developed by psychologists James Prochaska and Carlo DiClemente. This model explains that change isn't a single moment; it's a process that unfolds over time in six predictable stages.

1. **Precontemplation** – You're not even thinking about changing yet. You might not see a problem, or you feel stuck or hopeless about making a change.
2. **Contemplation** – You're aware that something needs to shift. You haven't committed to action yet, but you're thinking about the pros and cons of changing.
3. **Preparation** – You're getting ready to take action. You might start making small steps or plans, like researching or setting a start date (or like reading a self-help book).
4. **Action** – You're actively making changes. This is the phase where new behaviours are visible and intentional.
5. **Maintenance** – You're working to sustain the changes and to prevent relapse. This stage is about consistency, resilience, and adjusting when life throws curveballs
6. **Relapse** – Often included as a normal part of the process. Slipping back into old habits isn't failure, it's feedback. It's a chance to reflect, regroup, and return to the process with more awareness. This phase is where doing regular self-reflection is really useful!

What makes this model so powerful is that it shows us that change is rarely a straight line. We often move back and forth between stages and that's perfectly normal. Simply recognising where you are in the process can be empowering in itself. It encourages kindness and self-compassion while also giving you clarity on what's holding you back. And with that awareness comes motivation, the spark to take the next step forward because you can see both your progress and the stages where you might feel stuck.

The Grey Zone

A lot of people get stuck in the contemplation stage of change, and it can be incredibly difficult to move beyond it. In my experience, both personally and professionally, I've noticed that change often feels hardest when life is... well, fine. Not great, not terrible, just ticking along. The bills are being paid, the days are busy but manageable, and on the surface, everything seems okay. That's exactly what makes change so tricky in those moments.

Think about it. When in your life have you actually made significant changes? Most people don't change just because they feel like it. We tend to make real, lasting shifts when something big happens, that jolts us out of autopilot. Maybe it's a health scare, a diagnosis, the end of a relationship or the death of a loved one. Maybe you were made redundant, the house you were renting was suddenly sold, or you were forced to move because of a natural disaster. These are the kinds of external events that shake the ground beneath us and force us to act, because staying the same is no longer an option. I call this reactive change when change becomes necessary for survival, not just a preference.

But when life is just okay, when we're not deeply unhappy, just a little restless or dissatisfied. It's much easier to linger in the contemplation stage. We start to ask, "Is this it? Should I want more?" But there's no immediate urgency pushing us to act. There's no crisis demanding change, just a quiet internal whisper that something's off. This kind of change comes from within, and in many ways, it's the hardest kind. It is proactive change because it requires planning, motivation, courage, and a willingness to leave the familiar behind without a guaranteed payoff on the other side.

I've seen this contemplation stage in many of my clients. They come in saying they want something to shift, more purpose, more joy, more meaning, but they're not in crisis. They're in the grey zone. There's no immediate reason to take action because everything looks fine on paper and so it gets put on the back burner to deal with at another time. But that time never arrives. In this case change happens when the internal discomfort grows so strong, when the weight of 'fine' becomes unbearable, when they finally reach a tipping point and decide something has to give.

But the good news is change doesn't have to be dramatic or happen all at once. You don't need to wait until things reach a breaking point before you give yourself permission to take action. Real, lasting change is built step by step, through small, consistent choices made with intention. Each little shift moves you out of the grey zone and closer to the golden zone, where life feels lighter, clearer, and more aligned. When change is managed in this way, it becomes less overwhelming, more sustainable, and less disruptive to both you and the people around you. In addition, proactive change puts you in the driver's seat, giving you the autonomy and power to shape your own life at the pace that works for you.

The Pros And Cons Of Making Change

Before diving into big life changes or ones you're unsure about, it's useful to pause and explore the pros and cons of any such change. This simple but powerful exercise brings clarity and self-awareness to your decision-making process.

Change often feels exciting and hopeful, but it can also stir up fear, resistance or uncertainty. Taking time to examine and reflect candidly on the potential benefits and possible drawbacks can strengthen your motivation, prepare you for challenges, and even help you anticipate how others might respond.

Why This Works

Think of it as doing a little emotional and practical prep work before jumping in to action. When you understand what you stand to gain, what you may lose and what obstacles might come up, you're more likely to stay committed when the initial spark of motivation fades.

Writing down the pros helps you reconnect with your "why", the deeper reasons you're considering a change in the first place and allows you to visualise the positive impacts the change could have on your life.

Looking at the cons isn't about talking yourself out of making a change; it's about being realistic. It helps you identify potential hurdles, inner resistance or external pushback so you can plan ahead instead of being blindsided.

Here's a Simple Example

Let's say you're thinking about cutting back on alcohol during the week. Here's how this might play out:

Pros:
- I'll have more energy and feel clearer in the mornings.
- I'll sleep better.
- I'll save money.
- I'll feel more in control and aligned with my health goals.

Cons:
- I might feel left out at social events.
- Friends or family may question why I'm not drinking.
- I'll have to find new ways to wind down after a long day.
- It might be uncomfortable at first and take effort to stick with.

None of these cons are deal-breakers, but acknowledging them helps you prepare for any challenges that might arise and find practical ways to navigate them. For example, if you know friends might question your decision not to drink, you can think ahead about how you'll respond or perhaps find other ways to relax after work, like joining a gym.

Taking just five minutes to jot down a simple pros and cons list can bring surprising clarity. It allows you to plan and make change with a calm, thoughtful mindset rather than reacting out of emotion or impulse.

Tips For Building Habits That Last

So, how do you actually build sustainable habits into your life? Think of the steps ahead as gentle guidance, ideas to help you understand what makes change feel easier and more natural. Keep these tips in mind as you read because in chapter thirteen Let's Get Started: Your Slow Living Roadmap, you'll create your own slow living action plan and put these tips into practice.

Start Small: Pick Two Things That Resonate With You

Rather than trying to implement every change at once, start with two habits that are meaningful but easy to put into place. Focus on these first, and once they become second nature to you, introduce two more new habits, practising them until they too become second nature. Building habits is a process, and consistency matters more than speed. Slow, steady progress ensures that new behaviours not only become deeply ingrained in your routine but allow you to build your confidence in yourself as you achieve and live the new habits you create. As a rule of thumb, it can take a few weeks of consistent practice for a new habit to become established.

Reminders, Reminders, Reminders

I know I keep going on about them, but life gets busy, and even when we're eager to implement new habits, they can easily slip our minds. Using reminders keeps us motivated and on track. Some quick easy reminders include:

- Post-it notes in places you frequent, like on your bathroom mirror, back of the toilet door, fridge or work desk.
- Set your phone wallpaper or screensaver to an image or quote that reinforces your new habit.
- In unsupportive environments, find subtle reminders that work for you without drawing too much attention. A special image, keepsake, colour or animal.

Think of it like subliminal messaging; companies have used it for years to influence consumers, so why not use it to reinforce positive changes in your own life?

Habit Bundling: Pair a New Habit With an Existing One

Like we spoke about in earlier chapters, an effective way to make a new habit stick is to bundle it with something you already do. Attaching a new behaviour to an existing habit makes it easier to remember and naturally integrate into your routine. For example, set your intentions for the day in the shower or stretch or do deep breathing while waiting for your coffee to brew. By linking new habits to established ones, you make them feel less overwhelming and more sustainable.

Make It Easy For Yourself

If a habit requires too much effort to get started, you're less likely to follow through. Reduce barriers by making the habit as effortless as possible. For example, if you want to start journaling, keep your journal and pens in an easily accessible place instead of tucked away in a drawer. If you want to meditate in the morning, set up a cozy meditation spot so you don't have to prepare it each time. The easier it is, the more likely you are to stay consistent with it.

Create a Supportive Environment

Surround yourself with people who encourage your growth. Share your habit goals with supportive family and friends or join a group with similar aspirations. Reduce temptations that pull you away from your new habits (for example, if you want to read more, keep books visible and on hand or join a book club).

Be Kind to Yourself: Follow the 80/20 Rule

You're human, and some days will be harder than others. Instead of striving for perfection, adopt an 80/20 mindset. Aim to practice your habits 80% of the time and allow for 20% flexibility. Life happens, and some days won't go as planned.

Give yourself grace and compassion along the way. Progress will always matter more than perfection. If you have an off-day, or even an off-week, don't beat yourself up. Simply begin again, right where you are, and keep moving in your chosen direction. True sustainability comes from persistence, from the practice of returning to your path again and again, even when life throws you off course.

Not Everyone Will Cheer You On, And That's Okay

It's important to acknowledge that just because you're ready to make changes doesn't mean everyone in your life will be equally supportive, understanding, or thrilled about it. While that can be disappointing, or even hurtful, it's actually more common than you think.

People are complicated. As I mentioned earlier, we're all layered like onions, with old beliefs, roles, patterns and expectations wrapped around us, influencing our behaviour. Sometimes, when you start to peel back your layers and step into a new version of yourself, one that feels more aligned, balanced and peaceful, it can be confusing to others who are thrown off balance, not sure what to say or how to react to the new you.

Most of the time, people will support and cheer you on, which is great, but every now and then you might have some people in your life who aren't as enthusiastic as you would have hoped.

Why People Might Resist Your Change

Even when your intentions are positive, like setting healthier boundaries, slowing down, prioritising self-care, or saying no more often, people close to you might not know how to respond.

Sometimes it's because:
- They're used to a certain version of you, such as the people-pleaser, the go-getter, the fixer, the always-available one.
- Your change unintentionally shines a light on an area they're not ready to look at in themselves.
- They feel left out, confused, or even threatened by your shift, especially if it alters routines or roles in the relationship.
- They don't understand your reasons, especially if you haven't explained them clearly (or if they're not yet open to hearing them).
- Or it can be jealousy or competitiveness.

Sometimes, honestly, it's just human nature. We like predictability and, when someone starts growing, it can be unsettling for the people around them, even when that growth is beautiful and necessary.

Let's look at an example. Maybe you've decided to cut back on work commitments to create more time for rest and family. You're excited about this decision; it feels like a big step towards achieving a slower, more intentional life. But your partner, who's used to you being the productive one who brings in a certain income, might appear uneasy or even dismissive. Or your coworkers might joke about your new schedule, making comments like, "Must be nice to take it easy."

At first, it can feel like they don't support your growth. But often, these reactions have less to do with you and more to do with their own discomfort, jealousy, fear or unspoken expectations.

But it's important to remind yourself that this is your journey, not theirs. You don't need permission to grow. You don't need validation to want a calmer, more joyful life. And while it's lovely when others come along for the ride, they don't have to get it right away, or at all, for you to keep going.

What Can I Do?

If you're experiencing this kind of resistance or tension, here are a few things to keep in mind:

- Lead with compassion, not defensiveness. Change feels unsettling for everyone involved. Try to share your reasons with honesty and warmth when the timing feels right.
- Set clear but kind boundaries. You're allowed to protect the changes you're making, especially if they're improving your well-being.
- Surround yourself with supportive people. Seek out friends, mentors, or communities who do understand and uplift you.
- Let people adapt at their own pace. Some will come around when they see how grounded and happy you've become. Others may not and that's okay too.

You're not responsible for how others respond to your growth. What matters most is staying true to your own values, needs and vision for your life.

With time, many people do adjust. They start to see that the calmer, more present version of you isn't a threat; rather, it's an inspiration. And who knows? You might even quietly give them permission to seek a little more balance and peace in their own lives too.

Practical Exercise: Weighing The Pros And Cons of Change

Let's put a pros and cons list into practice. This simple exercise is a powerful way to set yourself up for success and move forward with more confidence and clarity.

Step 1: Pick One Small Change

What's one change you'd like to make in your life at the moment? Keep it simple.

Step 2: List the Pros

What benefits could this change bring—better energy, calmer moods, stronger relationships, more time?

Step 3: List the Cons

What might feel hard or inconvenient? Are the obstacles internal (like self-doubt) or external (like time, money, or other people's opinions)?

Step 4: Reflect

Which pros feel most motivating? Which cons are true barriers, and which are just temporary discomforts?

Step 5: Plan for Challenges

Jot down one or two ways you could soften or work around the cons.

Here's an example of what this exercise might look like for you:

Change I'd like to make: Write down three things I'm grateful for each day.

- **Pros:** More positivity, calmer mindset, noticing the good more naturally.
- **Cons:** Might forget, could feel repetitive, might feel silly.
- **Plan:** Set a reminder, vary the format, remind myself it's private and just for me.

Sometimes just seeing the pros and cons laid out clearly and having a plan for potential challenges is all it takes to move you forward with confidence.

Heartbeat Of The Chapter

Sustainable change isn't about quick fixes or drastic overhauls; it's about small, intentional shifts that build over time. Start with one or two changes, use reminders, bundle new habits with old ones, and set yourself up for success by making things easy. Most importantly, be patient with yourself. Growth is a lifelong process, and every small step you take brings you closer to a more mindful, intentional, and fulfilling life.

Remember, tomorrow is another day. Keep going, and trust that each small change is leading you toward something greater.

Challenge This Week

This week, set aside ten minutes to check in with yourself and think back to other changes you've made (or tried to make) in the past:

- What helped those changes stick?
- What made them challenging or short-lived?
- What lessons can you take from past changes you've made to support lasting, meaningful change now?

Remember awareness is the first step in creating real, sustainable change.

Affirmation This Week

"I am learning to stay committed to my growth, one choice at a time."

CHAPTER 12

When To Seek Professional Help

> "Until you make the unconscious conscious, it will direct your life and you will call it fate."
>
> - Carl Jung

Sometimes, personal change flows with ease. The people around you cheer you on. You begin making shifts that feel right and you're well on your way to the life you want to live. You feel proud, empowered, and supported.

But unfortunately, not all change feels smooth or simple.

Maybe you're trying to make positive changes, but those around you don't understand, or worse, they openly criticise or resist your efforts. Maybe everything seems fine on the outside, yet you feel disconnected, anxious, or unsettled on the inside. Or perhaps you simply feel stuck, despite your best intentions and efforts.

This is where speaking with a therapist, psychologist, or other trained professional can be incredibly helpful. While support from family and friends is valuable, there's something uniquely powerful about having a neutral, confidential space where you can explore your thoughts and feelings without judgment. A professional will help you untangle what's going on beneath the surface, reflect patterns you might not see, and gently guide you toward clarity and healing.

Here are some signs that working with a professional might be a useful step for you:

- You feel stuck in patterns you can't seem to shift, no matter how hard you try.
- You're struggling with a change you're trying to make or have made, and it's not feeling right.
- You feel emotionally overwhelmed, anxious, irritable, or low more often than not.
- You're having trouble understanding your emotions or reactions.
- You feel unsupported, misunderstood, or alone in your personal growth journey.

- You're navigating a major life transition, such as a divorce, grief, new parenting or a career shift.
- You're noticing the same issues or conflicts coming up in your relationships again and again.
- You want to explore past experiences or trauma that might still be affecting you.
- You're unsure of what you want or who you are anymore.
- You need a safe, judgment-free space to talk, reflect, and heal.

Seeking help isn't a sign of weakness. It's a sign of strength, self-awareness, and a commitment to your growth. Whether you talk to someone once or begin a longer journey of self-discovery, gaining support from a professional can be one of the most powerful and life-affirming things you can do for yourself.

How Can Therapy Help Me?

Now I might be biased here, but seeing a therapist does offer a wide range of benefits for your emotional, mental, and even physical well-being, including:

A Safe, Non-judgmental Space

Therapy provides a confidential, supportive environment where you can talk openly about anything, without fear of being judged or misunderstood. You don't have to filter your thoughts or worry about burdening others. It's a space dedicated just to you, to be able to talk about whatever you need to.

Increased Self-Awareness

Therapists are trained to help you explore patterns in your thinking, emotions and behaviour. This deeper awareness helps you understand why you do what you do and empowers you to make more intentional choices.

Emotional Regulation

Through therapy, you learn how to identify, understand and manage your emotions. It gives you the tools to stay grounded and learn to cope with your feelings rather than becoming overwhelmed or trying to avoid them.

Better Relationships

By improving your communication skills, setting healthy boundaries, and understanding your own relational patterns, therapy can help you develop stronger, healthier relationships with others, whether they're your partner, your children, or friends and colleagues.

Personal Growth and Clarity

You don't need to be in crisis to benefit from therapy. Some of the most meaningful growth happens when life feels steady, and you're simply seeking more clarity, direction, or a deeper connection with yourself. Therapy can help you tune into your values, goals, and purpose, and support you in living with greater intention and authenticity. Think of it as self-reflection on steroids!

Finding The Right Therapist

Finding the right therapist may feel a bit daunting at first, but it's worth the effort. The therapeutic relationship plays a big role in how effective therapy is, so it's important to find someone you feel comfortable talking to, who you can be open with, and who will understand, encourage and support you.

Here's a guide to help you find the right therapist for you:

Know What You're Looking For

Start by getting clear on why you're seeking therapy.

- Are you dealing with anxiety, stress, depression, grief, relationship issues, trauma, or something else?
- Do you want short-term, goal-focused therapy or longer-term exploration and healing?
- Do you prefer someone who offers practical tools, or someone who listens and reflects more deeply?

Knowing what you want will assist you to narrow your search and find someone who aligns with your needs.

Explore the Different Types of Therapy

Therapists draw from a wide range of therapeutic approaches, each offering unique tools and perspectives. Some of the common forms of therapy include:

- **Cognitive Behavioural Therapy (CBT)** which helps identify and change unhelpful thoughts and behaviours, often used for anxiety, depression, and stress.
- **Psychodynamic Therapy** which delves into past experiences, childhood dynamics, and unconscious patterns that may still be influencing you today.
- **Humanistic or Person-Centred Therapy** is rooted in empathy, acceptance, and authenticity. This approach supports personal growth, self-understanding, and emotional healing.
- **Acceptance and Commitment Therapy (ACT)** encourages psychological flexibility by helping you accept difficult emotions and commit to meaningful values-based actions.
- **Dialectical Behaviour Therapy (DBT)** which is especially effective for emotional regulation and interpersonal issues, combining CBT with mindfulness and distress tolerance skills.

Naturally, you are not expected to become an instant expert on these various therapies. However, having brief general knowledge about them may help in pointing you in the right direction. It's also worth noting that many therapists don't confine themselves to one approach. Instead, they use an eclectic or integrative style, drawing from different methods to tailor a personalised plan that fits their clients' needs, preferences, and goals.

Therapy works best when it's a collaborative process, and finding the right fit is part of that journey.

Ask the Right Questions

Once you've found a few potential therapists, don't be afraid to ask questions like:

- What training and experience do you have working with [your concern]?
- What's your general approach or style in therapy?
- What can I expect in a typical session?
- Most therapists are happy to answer these questions.

Consider Logistics

Think about:

- Location – Do you want someone nearby or are you open to online therapy?
- Delivery method – Do they offer face-to-face appointments, over the phone and/or online appointments?
- Availability – Can they see you at times that fit your schedule?
- Cost – What's the fee per session? Do they offer sliding scale pricing? Are they covered by government rebates or private health insurance?

Trust Your Gut

After the first session or two, ask yourself:

- Did I feel heard and understood?
- Was I comfortable opening up?

- Did I feel respected, not judged?
- Did I get a sense that this therapist gets me?

If not, it's completely okay to try someone else. Good therapists won't take it personally; therapy is about you, not them.

Use Trusted Directories and Recommendations

You can find therapists through:

- Psychology Today, Therapy Route, or GoodTherapy.org
- National directories like Australian Psychological Society (APS), British Association of Counselling and Psychotherapy (BACP), American Psychological Association (APA)
- Word of mouth, ask trusted friends, your family doctor, or other professionals
- Many workplaces have an employee assistance program that offers confidential counselling
- Community mental health centres or online therapy platforms (like BetterHelp.com (worldwide), Talkspace.com (US))

Finding the right therapist can take time. You deserve someone who feels like a good fit for you, someone you can grow with, feel safe with, and be yourself with.

How Often Should I Go?

The duration and intervals of therapy varies from person to person. Some people find that just one session is enough to get the clarity they need, while others benefit from regular ongoing support. There's no one-size-fits-all answer; it depends on your goals, needs, and what feels most helpful to you. This is something you can openly discuss with your therapist and work out together as you go.

Therapy As A Tool For Slow Living

Now don't get me wrong, you don't have to engage in therapy to stop rushing and start living a slower, less stressful and more enjoyable life. But if this a tool that might work for you, for some of the reasons listed earlier, then it can be a powerful and empowering experience.

When you work with a therapist, you're carving out space in your life to slow down and reflect. You're intentionally stepping off the hamster wheel to look inward, examining old habits, questioning beliefs that no longer serve you, and gently untangling the emotional clutter that gets in the way of living with clarity and peace. Rather than rushing to fix, achieve, or "get it right," therapy encourages you to be curious, compassionate and grounded in your growth.

For many who are used to caring for others and pushing through overwhelm, therapy becomes a sacred pause, a chance to ask, "What do I need?" and

"What do I want?". It's a space where you're allowed to slow down and meet yourself, right where you are.

Heartbeat Of The Chapter

It's natural for us to think and act with care and compassion toward others, yet far less common to extend that same kindness to ourselves. We often push ourselves to exhaustion before even considering asking for help, when, in truth, reaching out is one of the most self-compassionate things we can do. Asking for help opens the door to the support we need to regain balance, set meaningful goals, and take positive steps toward a more fulfilling life.

Whether you're navigating major life transitions, struggling with emotions that don't seem to shift, or simply craving deeper clarity and personal growth, therapy offers a powerful space for healing, self-discovery, and meaningful change.

Challenge This Week

This week, I invite you to pause and reflect on the support network in your life right now:

- Who are the people you can rely on?
- Do you have friends, family members or colleagues who encourage your growth and support your journey?

- Are there people who uplift you, hold space for you, or simply listen without judgment?

If the answer is yes, that's amazing! Take a moment to feel grateful for those connections. Maybe even reach out and let them know how much their support means to you.

If the answer is no, or if your support system feels a little shaky, that's okay. You're not alone, and there are always ways to build new, supportive connections. Consider these words to be your nudge to explore:

- Can you join an online group or community of like-minded people working toward similar goals?
- Is there a local meetup group, class, book club, or wellness group that is aligned with your values?
- Could you benefit from professional support, like speaking with a therapist or life coach?

Connection is a core part of slow living because we don't grow well in isolation. Surround yourself with people (online or offline) who believe in your ability to change. It can make all the difference.

Affirmation This Week

"I am learning to honour my own personal needs, seek support when I need it, and grow with courage and compassion."

CHAPTER 13

Let's Get Started: Your Slow Living Roadmap

"Success is the sum of small efforts, repeated day in and day out."

– Robert Collier

You did it! Congratulations on making it this far! Before we dive into planning your next steps and putting the knowledge and insights you've learnt into practice, let's take a moment to reflect and recap everything we've covered so far.

In Chapter 1: Slow Living: What it is and Isn't, we looked at the myths, misconceptions and the guiding principles of slow living. This chapter dispelled common myths and highlighted how slow living is a mindset that anyone can adopt, at any age, to create a more fulfilling, balanced and joyful life.

In Chapter 2: Living Life on Purpose: The Power of Intention, we discovered how, at the heart of slow living, is the practice of setting clear intentions. Rather than moving through life on autopilot, this chapter explores how conscious decision-making can transform the way we approach our daily routines, relationships, and goals. When we live with intention, we create more meaning, reduce stress, and cultivate a deeper sense of purpose.

In Chapter 3: Right Here, Right Now: The Power of Presence, we covered how one of the greatest gifts of slow living is the ability to experience the fullness of each moment. We discussed the importance of mindfulness in daily activities, conversations, or simple pleasures, and how by breaking free from the cycle of distraction and multitasking, we learn to savour life's small joys and create lasting, meaningful experiences.

In Chapter 4: Everyday Grace: Finding Joy and Gratitude in the Ordinary, we looked at how gratitude is a powerful tool for shifting our perspective and deepening our appreciation for life. We discovered that gratitude helps us cultivate inner peace, even when we are struggling with difficulties and hardships in our lives.

In Chapter 5: Self-Care: The Art of Looking After You, we learnt that self-care is not indulgent, it's necessary. Here, you were encouraged to shift your mindset from reactive to restorative care, tending to your needs regularly so you can show up for yourself and others more fully. This chapter assisted you to redefine self-care as essential and provided guidelines on how to develop your own self-care menu.

In Chapter 6: Simplify, Unclutter and Thrive, we looked at how simplifying is about clearing the clutter, not just in your physical space, but also in your calendar, mind, and heart. This chapter helped you identify what's essential and what's simply noise. By letting go of the unnecessary, you create more room for calmness, clarity, and connection, allowing your life to feel lighter and more intentional.

In Chapter 7: Disconnecting to Reconnect: The Path Back to You, we looked at how, in a world of constant connectivity, we often lose touch with ourselves and those closest to us. This chapter encouraged you to step back from screens and distractions and reconnect with the present moment, your loved ones, and your inner world

In Chapter 8: The Power of Boundaries: Making Space for What Matters, we explored the power of setting healthy boundaries as a way to protect your time, energy, and emotional well-being. You learned how to say no without guilt, define your limits with compassion, and give yourself permission to prioritise what's important to you.

In Chapter 9: Learning to Let Go, we acknowledged that letting go is one of the hardest and most liberating parts of slow, intentional living. This chapter guided you through the emotional process of how to let go with practical exercises to help you along the way. By letting go, you create space for healing, growth, and more authentic living.

In Chapter 10: The Power of Self-Reflection, we explored tools for you to tune into your thoughts and emotions. By asking thoughtful questions and creating space for regular check-ins, you give yourself the opportunity to make adjustments on the go and acknowledge the progress you've made in your journey.

In Chapter 11: Making Lasting Change, we looked at what it takes to create change that sticks. This chapter guided you through the natural stages of change, highlighting the importance of readiness, patience, and self-compassion along the way.

In Chapter 12: When to Seek Professional Help, we acknowledged that while self-help tools are powerful, sometimes extra support is helpful. This chapter offered guidance on recognising when you might need professional support, what therapy can offer, and how to find the right therapist for you. You were reminded that seeking help is a strength, not a weakness and that you don't have to do this alone.

From Ideas To Action

You've come a long way through this book, exploring new ideas, insights, and ways of seeing your life. Now it's time to bring all of that in to reality in a way that feels real and achievable for you. One of the best ways to begin is by creating your own personal action plan, something simple, flexible, and grounded in what matters most to you. A roadmap to guide your journey.

Think of this roadmap as a living framework to help you turn your slow living intentions into meaningful, sustainable actions. It's not about perfection, strict routines, or doing everything at once. It's about giving yourself a starting point, a foundation you can grow from.

Use it to check in with yourself, celebrate your progress, and stay connected to your values and goals.

Most of all, let it remind you that slow living is a journey, not a race. Take what serves you, leave what doesn't, and allow your plan to grow and evolve with you as you create a life filled with more presence, clarity, joy, and fulfilment.

Now, let's begin!

Your Slow Living Roadmap

1. Define Your Why

Let's take a moment to pause and connect with your reasons for wanting a slower, more intentional life.

Why do you want to embrace slow living? (Dig deep, be as detailed as possible in your answer)

For example: I want to stop feeling like I'm constantly rushing through my life. I want to feel calmer in my body and more present with my family. I'm tired of multitasking and missing the small moments that actually bring me joy. I want to live in a way that feels aligned with what matters to me, more time in nature, more time for creativity, more flow in my days.

2. Where Are You Now?

Think about the different areas of your life, your social life, family life, work life, relationships, physical health and spiritual connection.

What areas of your life feel rushed, overwhelming, or out of sync? (For example: My workday is constantly overbooked, I'm always on my phone at home, my home feels chaotic.)

What areas of your life already feel intentional, grounded, or joyful? (For example: Eating dinner without screens, I have a good social group, going for walks with my partner, I have a good connection with my kids.)

3. Revisit the Principles of Slow Living

Let's take a moment to quickly revisit each principle and reflect on what truly resonated with you throughout this book or through your own research and experimentation. Maybe you've already tried a few strategies as you worked through the chapters, or perhaps you've been reading and thinking about what you'd like to explore next.

Either way, by reflecting you will notice what felt useful, what sparked curiosity, and what you're excited to bring into your life. This step is about turning insights into actions and giving yourself a chance to make these ideas real.

Intention

- Looking back, what have you noticed about how setting an intention influences your day or choices?

- If you haven't tried it yet, what kind of intention would you like to start with?

Mindfulness
- What mindfulness practices have you tried or found helpful?
- If you're just getting started, which practices sound most approachable or enjoyable to begin with?

Gratitude
- Which gratitude practices felt meaningful or easy to maintain?
- Or which gratitude habits feel like a natural first step for you?

Decluttering & Simplifying
- What spaces or parts of your life already feel lighter or more organised?
- What area (physical, mental, or emotional) could you simplify next?

Self-Care
- What self-care activities do you want to commit to regularly?

Reconnecting
- What habits or experiences help you feel most connected to yourself, others, or nature?
- If you've been feeling disconnected, what steps could help you reconnect?

Setting Boundaries

- Are there any areas of your life you need to set boundaries in?
- If yes what are the boundaries?
- How will you communicate them? (tell others or keep them to yourself)

Letting Go

- Are there any habits or beliefs you need to let go of?
- What things are out of your control that you need to shift your attitude about?
- What letting-go practices have helped you or would you like to try?

Self-Reflection

- How will you create more space for self-reflection?
- What are your go-to self-reflection questions?

4. Choose Your Starting Principles

Now that you've looked back over each principle and reflected on what felt most useful or what you'd still like to try, let's use that information to help you choose two slow living principles you'd like to start building into your life.

When you're starting something new, it's best to begin with small, manageable steps rather than big, emotionally demanding ones. Choose changes that feel light and doable, ones that fit easily into your life right now. Starting with what feels gentle helps you build confidence and consistency. Just like we touched on in the chapter on how to make lasting change, if you take on too much too soon, it can quickly become overwhelming and make it harder to stay motivated.

Think of these first steps as gentle experiments, simple ways to ease into change and build trust in yourself and the process. Remember, small steps create momentum, and momentum leads to meaningful change.

Which two principles do you want to start with?

5. Create Your Action Plan

Now let's make it real. For each principle, define a clear intention and actions you can take to bring it to life. You will also look at the pros and cons of each action and how you can set yourself up for success. Below is an example of how this might look.

Principle #1: Mindfulness

My intention is:
I want to be more present during the small, everyday moments, especially around my family.

Action step:

I'll put my phone on silent and place it in another room during dinner and the hour before bedtime. This will help me focus on being with my family; really listening when my kids are talking; and becoming more aware of how I'm feeling at the end of the day.

What are the pros and cons of this action?

Pros:

I'll feel more connected and present with my family.

I'll be able to wind down easier in the evenings.

I'll be setting a positive example around screen use for the kids.

Cons:

I might feel the urge to check messages out of habit.

It could feel uncomfortable at first, like I'm missing something important.

How can I set myself up to succeed?

Put a basket in the hallway where phones go after 6:30 p.m.

Use the "Do Not Disturb" feature on my phone and only let important contacts through.

I'll tell the family what my plan is so they can help support me.

Keep a journal nearby to jot down thoughts or to-dos that pop up, so I don't feel like I have to reach for my phone.

I'll put reminders up in the kitchen so I don't forget until it becomes an automatic habit.

Your Turn:

Principle #1: ....

My intention is: ....

....

....

Action step: ....

....

....

....

What are the pros and cons of this action?

....

....

....

....

How can I set myself up to succeed?

....

....

....

....

Principle #2: ....

My intention is: ....

....

....

Action step: ....

....

....

....

What are the pros and cons of this action?

....

....

....

....

How can I set myself up to succeed?

....

....

....

....

6. My Personal Affirmation

To help you stay motivated, create a personal affirmation that connects you back to your intention. You can choose one from this book or come up with your own.

Then place it somewhere you'll see it often, on your mirror, in your journal, or as a phone wallpaper, so it reminds you of what you're trying to do. You can make a few affirmations if you like, but don't overdo it, one or two is a great place to start.

7. Tracking Progress and Adjusting

After trying out your action plan for a few weeks, it's helpful to pause and check in with yourself. This is where your self-reflection practice starts to shine.

What's flowing well? What feels off or forced? Reflect on what's working, what needs tweaking, and how your slow living practices are (or aren't) supporting the life you want to create.

Remember, there's no one-size-fits-all formula here. Everyone's version of slow living will be different and that's exactly how it should be. Your plan is meant to reflect your values, energy, stage of life, and unique rhythm. This isn't about judgment, it's about gentle course correction, deepening your self-awareness and acknowledging what's working well.

Ask yourself:
- What changes have I noticed in my mindset or lifestyle since starting this journey?

- What challenges have come up, and do I need to adjust my approach?

When you feel ready to expand your slow living practice, simply revisit the "Create your action plan" section and add in the new principles or ideas.

Keep this plan where you can see it and revisit it often. Use it as a flexible, living guide that will grow and evolve with you. Some days you'll make big strides, other days just small steps, but it all counts, and remember the 80/20 rule. Try your best 80% of the time, and the other 20%, well, life happens, so show yourself some compassion and understanding.

With your roadmap now in place, it's time to get honest about the one factor that ultimately determines your success: your own choices and responsibility.

It's Time For Some Tough Love

I hate to be the bad guy here, truly I do, but I need to say this clearly and with love: your happiness, your growth, and the life you want to create are your responsibility. No one else's.

There. I said it.

Good thing I waited until the end of the book to drop this truth bomb. If I'd led with it, you might've thrown the whole thing across the room! But if you've made it this far, you're ready to hear it. And you need to hear it. Because it's true.

No matter what you've been through, and I say this with deep compassion for whatever pain, trauma, or challenges that life has handed you, there comes a point when we each have to step up and take ownership of our actions, our choices, and ultimately, our future. It doesn't mean what happened to you wasn't unfair or unjust. It doesn't mean you deserved it or that you should just get over it. But it does mean that healing and moving positively into your future is now in your hands.

You are the only one who can make the changes needed to create a better life for yourself. No one is coming to save you. No one else can do the inner work, the hard choices, or the uncomfortable growth for you. It's yours. As confronting as that may be, it is also incredibly empowering, because it means you're not powerless. You get to steer the ship from here.

This truth, this idea that it's all on me, was not easy for me to accept either. I didn't exactly high-five myself when I realised it. In fact, I resisted it for years. I mean, helping other people find their truth? Sure. That was easy. But looking in the mirror and saying, "Well, if you don't do it for yourself, no one else will... so let's get going," that was a moment of reckoning.

So, here's your invitation to take your power back. Stop waiting. Stop outsourcing your joy. Stop waiting for this or that to happen before you live your life or make changes. This is your life, and no one else can live it for you. So keep going, keep adjusting, and above all, be kind to yourself as you walk this beautiful, slow path. You are already on your way!

Affirmation This Week

"I am learning to honour the pace of my own becoming. I trust that slow, intentional steps will carry me exactly where I'm meant to go. I release the pressure to rush, and welcome the quiet power of presence, peace, and purpose."

CHAPTER 14

Final Thoughts

As you read the final pages of this book, I want to remind you of something simple but powerful:

You don't have to have it all figured out. You just have to begin.

Living a slower, more intentional life isn't about perfection. It's about presence. It's about tuning in, making small conscious choices, and continuing to come back to what matters, again and again.

Maybe as you read this book, you had moments of insight or relief. Maybe you saw yourself in the stories or exercises. Maybe you felt inspired or maybe you felt overwhelmed. All of that is okay. This book isn't a checklist to complete. It's an invitation. A permission slip. A companion for the parts of you that are drained by the rushing, striving or feeling like life is passing you by too quickly.

I hope you walk away with the knowledge that real change doesn't have to be dramatic to be meaningful. The quiet choices, the deep breath before reacting, the moment you pause to feel the sunshine on your face, the boundary you set to protect your energy: these are acts of self-respect and self-love. These are the bricks that build a slower, happier, more fulfilling life.

Let yourself return to this work whenever you need. Revisit the challenges. Reread the affirmations. Keep reflecting. Keep connecting. Keep choosing presence over pressure.

Most of all, be gentle with yourself. Growth is never a straight line. Some days you'll soar. Some days you'll slip. Both are part of the journey. What matters is that you keep showing up with honesty, intention, and love.

Thank you for letting me walk alongside you.

You're already doing better than you think.

And the best part?

This is just the beginning!

NOTE TO THE READER

From the bottom of my heart, thank you for reading this book.

My sincerest hope is that it has helped you slow down, reconnect with what truly matters, and begin shaping a life that feels less rushed and more meaningful. Whether it sparked big changes or gently planted seeds that will blossom over time, I'm so grateful you took this journey with me.

Slow living isn't a destination; it's a practice. A way of being. A mindset. Some days it flows with ease, and other days it takes conscious effort. Be kind to yourself as you continue walking this path. Even the smallest shift in how you show up is a powerful step.

I'd love to hear from you, whether it's your thoughts on this book, feedback about what resonated (or didn't), or a reflection on how your own slow living journey is unfolding. Your insights and experiences matter, and I invite you to reach out and share them with me at

Email: slowdownwithliz@gmail.com

And if this book resonated with you, please leave a review on Amazon or Goodreads. I'd be deeply grateful and it helps others find their way to this work.

You can also connect with me online, where I share regular inspiration, techniques and reminders to slow down and live with intention.

- **Facebook:** @slowdownwithliz
- **Instagram:** @slowdownwithliz
- **YouTube:** @slowdownwithliz
- **Website:** www.slowdownwithliz.com

Let this be the beginning of a beautiful, slower, more soul-nourishing chapter of your life. I'm cheering you on, every step of the way.

With love and deep gratitude,

Liz

REFERENCES

Calm Blog. (n.d.). *The power of setting intentions & how to set mindful ones.* [online] Available at: https://www.calm.com/blog/setting-intentions.

Emmons, R.A. and Crumpler, C.A. (2000). Gratitude as a Human Strength: Appraising the Evidence. *Journal of Social and Clinical Psychology*, 19(1), pp.56–69. doi:https://doi.org/10.1521/jscp.2000.19.1.56.

Keng, S.L., Smoski, M.J. and Robins, C.J. (2011). Effects of Mindfulness on Psychological Health: a Review of Empirical Studies. *Clinical Psychology Review*, [online] 31(6), pp.1041–1056. doi:https://doi.org/10.1016/j.cpr.2011.04.006.

Kondo, M. (2015). *The Life-changing Magic of Tidying Up.* Thorndike Press.

Lopez, S.J. and Snyder, C.R. (2002). *Handbook of Positive Psychology.* New York; Oxford: Oxford University Press.

Prochaska, J.O., DiClemente, C.C. and Norcross, J.C. (1992). In search of how people change: Applications to addictive behaviors. *American Psychologist*, [online] 47(9), pp.1102–1114. doi:https://doi.org/10.1037//0003-066x.47.9.1102.

Tseng, J. and Poppenk, J. (2020). Brain meta-state transitions demarcate thoughts across task contexts exposing the mental noise of trait neuroticism. *Nature Communications*, [online] 11(1), p.3480. doi:https://doi.org/10.1038/s41467-020-17255-9.

Voyage New York. (2024). *The Slow Living Movement: Prioritizing Mindfulness and Intentionality - Voyage New York*. [online] Available at: https://voyageny.com/the-slow-living-movement-prioritizing-mindfulness-and-intentionality/.

Worldhappiness.report. (2025). *World Happiness Report 2025: People are much kinder than we expect, research shows*. [online] Available at: tps://worldhappiness.report/news/world-happiness-report-2025-people-are-much-kinder-than-we-expect-research-shows/.

www.collective-genius.com. (n.d.). *The history of SMART Goals and OKRs*. [online] Available at: https://www.collective-genius.com/blog/the-history-of-smart-goals-and-okrs.

www.ingramcontent.com/pod-product-compliance
Lightning Source LLC
Chambersburg PA
CBHW020523080526
44583CB00013B/719